D1481167

THE TAO AND CHINESE CULTURE

da liu

SCHOCKEN BOOKS • NEW YORK

First published by SCHOCKEN BOOKS 1979
10 9 8 7 6 5 4 3 2   82

Copyright © 1979 by Da Liu

Library of Congress Cataloging in Publication Data

Liu, Da.
 .The Tao and Chinese culture.

 Bibliography: p.
 Includes index.
 1.   Taoism.   I.   Title.
BL1920.L56   299' .514   78–26767

Manufactured in the United States of America

ISBN 0-8052-3714-3 (hardback)
       0-8052-0702-3 (paperback)

CONTENTS

PREfACE

Accounts of Taoist ideas and practices can be found in many writings by Sinologists, and numerous Western-language translations of the Taoist classics are now available. But although some of these have considerable merit, they have not sufficiently revealed the true significance of the Taoist tradition in Chinese thought and civilization. The prevalent historical view of Taoism among Western students of Chinese culture today is that while it produced some beautiful and profound writings in ancient times, Taoism became politically overshadowed by Confucianism during and after the Han dynasty and later developed a curious mixture of superstitions and religious rituals that mainly imitated the practices of Buddhism. Such a perspective on Taoism and its historical evolution in China is both distorted and highly oversimplified. Yet considering the process by which the Western world has learned about Chinese culture, it is not very surprising that this view has become widely accepted.

For one thing, the historical perspective on China available to the West has made it quite difficult to recognize and identify the specifically Taoist aspects of its culture. By the time the first Europeans arrived in China during the seventeenth century, the religious practices of Taoism and Buddhism had been thoroughly

mixed together for at least a millennium, and the official orthodoxy
of Confucianism in government and society had dominated Chinese
history since before the birth of Christ. The orthodox Confucianists
who compiled the historical records of China had neither the
knowledge nor the inclination to give an accurate account of Taoist
ideas and their influence.

Thus, an authentic account of Taoist history was not to be found
in writing but survived mainly in the oral tradition among the people.
Western scholars, unfortunately, have always been hindered by this
imbalance, especially since most were more sympathetic to the
skeptical rationalism of the Confucianist scholars than to the
sometimes wild peculiarities of those who had detailed knowledge of
other philosophical viewpoints. Most have been unaware of the full
extent to which their views of Chinese cultural history were left
incomplete as a result. Some Western writers, especially Joseph
Needham, have given remarkably perceptive accounts of Taoism in
spite of the difficulties of obtaining information. But, such efforts
notwithstanding, an accurate treatment of traditional Chinese culture
based on a full understanding of the Taoist tradition in its own terms
is still unavailable to the Western reader.

There is a real need today for better understanding of the Taoist
tradition, not only because of its importance for the adequate
appreciation of Chinese civilization, but also because it represents an
approach to life and to the universe that can have immense value for
dealing with the problems of the modern world. Yet this book does
not attempt to proselytize for Taoism. My task has been guided by
the conviction that if the ideas and practices of Taoism are presented
as faithfully as possible, the wisdom contained in them will naturally
become apparent and their benefits will gradually achieve widespread
recognition.

It is a task for which I have prepared since my early youth, when
I grew up near Suchow, in a region of China of great historical
importance for Taoism, where the Taoist tradition was at that time
still a strong influence in the lives of the people. Over a period of
many years, my knowledge of Taoism has grown through the
continual study of a large number of original Chinese writings on the
subject, as well as the cultivation of practical Taoist techniques. This

book is the outcome of my own experience, in addition to a great deal of research. Throughout, I have made an effort to document the sources of my information insofar as necessary in a popular work. In particular, I have tried to refer to sources in English when available, not merely to aid the reader but also to record my indebtedness to those works in English which I have read and found useful. Regarding my quotations from the classic writings of Chuang Tzu and Lao Tzu, which have been translated in so many different ways, although I have studied many of the available translations, I almost always developed my own translations for the purpose of quotation, concluding that my own reading of the original Chinese was a better guide to the real meaning of the passages than any of the English versions I found. In my footnotes, however, I indicate for each passage one or more translations I have found interesting, referring the reader to alternative versions for purposes of comparison.

Many people assisted me in the preparation of this book. I would like to thank John Lad, Jim Hickey, Rosemary Birardi, Liz Birardi, Kibbie Payne, Kwang-Fu Chu, William F. C. Chao, Chia Lin Song, Steven Berko, C. T. Chang, Kao Liu Yu-Ying, and Basil Condos.

CHAPTER 1
INTRODUCTION

Western scholars have often sought to define Tao by studying the classic writings of Lao Tzu—whose *Tao Te Ching* ranks with the Bible as one of the ancient texts most frequently subjected to translation and conjecture. Translators of Lao Tzu have described Tao with various words: Way, Path, Nature, Mind, Reason, Truth, Logos, Law, God, even "undifferentiated aesthetic continuum." Collectively, these would-be synonyms imply a common approach to Tao, but none adequately conveys its basic meaning.

Part of the difficulty arises because Tao is vital to those timeless teachings of Chinese religion, philosophy, and the humanities that are unfamiliar to the occidental layman. More to the point, however, Tao is not just for the intellectual elite. Instead, the meaning of Tao exists in Chinese everyday life as an omnipresent ubiquitous awareness grasped by even the poorest peasant. In this light, "Tao" is like other words that are so basic to us they defy simple definition— like "goodness," "wrong," or "freedom," yet whose profound meanings we understand, though perhaps only viscerally. Since such words contribute to the foundation of our beliefs and arts, we must continually test our understanding of them through direct experience as well as through the study of writings on them.

It is not unreasonable to expect that similar effort can enhance the Westerner's understanding of Tao. In practice, however, it is not so easy. The process of understanding "goodness" begins at an early age for members of all cultures. However, it is assumed that the reader of this book has not had the chance to observe and test first-hand the experiential definition of Tao. Even a trip to China would not ensure success, for that nation's recent history has seriously threatened the survival of practices and beliefs once common to traditional Chinese culture.

This book, then, provides an understanding of—and, in so doing, helps preserve—authentic elements of Chinese culture within the unifying context of Tao.

One commonly hears Tao referred to as if it were a definite established entity: *the* Tao. Granted, it is occasionally difficult to avoid this practice, but the tendency can be misleading. Fundamentally, Tao is everywhere, in all things, at all times. It is no one thing to the exclusion of all others. If Tao is a name, it designates "all-ness"; to speak of *the* Tao, therefore, is to encompass the universe.

The use of the article "the" identifies Tao as a noun—the name of *an* object, *a* place or condition. But such a grammatical classification is imprecise. Not only may Tao be used as a noun, verb, or adjective, but its meaning may be determined according to the context in which it is used. "Tao li," for example, stands for "rationality," whereas "Tao yi" means "rightness" and "Jen Tao" "kindness." Other examples can be found in Japanese words, such as the names attributed to their martial arts (judo, aikido, and so on) which contain "do" as a part.

Tao, then, is too universal a term to be restricted by a conventional use of "the". Indeed, the very first sentence of Lao Tzu's *Tao Te Ching* identifies the futility of such labeling:

> The Tao that can be spoken of
> Is not the real Tao.[1]

The spoken word limits Tao to a merely phonic rather than total experience. It is the nature of language to codify organic experience into frozen categories. Once jacketed, a growing and vital reality may too easily be stored away as an intellectual abstraction and ultimately forgotten or dismissed. In this sense, the nature of language is ill-suited to the nature of Tao.

Tao is an on-going process of participation and discovery. Later chapters of the *Tao Te Ching*, therefore, refer to Tao as "vague," "mysterious," "hidden," "unknown," "unfathomable," "nameless"[2]— that which is known only through perpetual encounter.

Let us begin, then, by acknowledging that the *Tao Te Ching* itself distinguishes between the word "Tao" and the notion of namelessness:

> It is from the unnamed Tao
> That Heaven and Earth sprang;
> The named is but
> The Mother of the ten thousand creatures.[3]

This suggests that the word "Tao" may be used to emphasize certain aspects of the entity at the expense of others.

This premise is supported in the *I Ching*, a text as fundamental to the ancient Chinese religious traditions of Taoism and Confucianism as the Old and New Testaments are to the Judaeo-Christian teachings. A passage from *Ta Chuan* (The Great Treatise), dating from the time of Confucius, contains this insight about the nature of Tao:

> The kind man discovers it and calls it kind.
> The wise man discovers it and calls it wise.
> The common people use it every day
> And are not aware of it.[4]

Not merely do different people understand Tao differently, what each person finds in the Tao depends on and, in some sense, reflects his own character. Thus Tao is somewhat like a mirror, in that it reflects the perceiver and his or her context.

This conclusion, if understood correctly, does not imply that people cannot communicate about Tao. On the contrary, it stresses the value of such communication for helping people understand one another. In addition, the classic writings of ancient China discuss Tao as a source of insight into the character and world view of a major civilization. Understanding these classics of wisdom and cultural heritage, valuable in itself, can be a guide to the significance of Tao within that heritage.

It is not known for certain when the word "Tao" was first used in China. In all likelihood, it was part of the spoken language long before it appeared in writing. The most ancient writing in which it can be found is the *Shu Ching*, a classic collection of historical documents. For example, the Emperor Shun (2255–2205 B.C.) reportedly gave the following advice to his minister Yu, who shortly afterward became his successor:

> The human mind is dangerous—its selfish tendencies lead to error and crime, and its affinity for Tao is small.[5]

This remark reflects aspects of Tao that have since been detailed in later writings. Tao, being opposed to selfishness and wrong, represents a moral ideal, which is not strongly inherent in man. Tao may grow in man, but not with the hearty abundance of the wild grasses; rather, it is more like a delicate flower that must be carefully nurtured if it is to survive.

"The Great Treatise" of the *I Ching* is another ancient resource for our study. In this commentary on the *kua* (trigram and hexagram symbols) and their significance, Tao refers to that underlying reality on which the entire symbolic system of the *I Ching* is based:

> That which lets now the dark, now the light appear is Tao.[6]

Here, light and dark refer to Yang and Yin, the two funda-mental, complementary, opposite cosmic forces through which the the various forms of I ("change") are symbolically represented. The trigrams and hexagrams of the *I Ching* consist of line drawings: The unbroken lines stand for Yang and the broken lines Yin. There are eight three-lined figures (trigrams) and sixty-four six-lined figures (hexagrams), which have been determined by all the possible (linear) permutations of Yin and Yang lines. Thus, the quote links all change in the cosmos to Tao.

The trigrams and hexagrams had symbolic relevance for divination purposes several centuries before the writing of "The Great Treatise." But the above quote suggests that Tao cannot be understood as any particular combination of Yin and Yang; rather, Tao exists as the constant interaction between the two cosmic principles of change, allowing it to continue in all things. As such, Tao is that on which everything in the *I Ching* depends.

"The Great Treatise" states this explicitly:

> The *I Ching* is a book vast and great, in which everything is completely contained. The Tao of heaven is in it, the Tao of earth is in it, and the Tao of man is in it. It combines these three primal powers and doubles them; that is why there are six lines [in each hexagram]. The six lines are nothing other than the Tao of the three primal powers.[7]

There are many other places in "The Great Treatise" in which "Tao" is used in compounds with other words—for instance, "Tao of day and night," "Tao of the sun and moon," "Tao of the ancient kings." These expressions refer to levels of symbolism in the trigrams and hexagrams that describe various natural and social situations.

The use of these symbols affected many aspects of life in ancient China. Methods of interpreting and applying the ideograms developed over several centuries, so that more than one tradition of interpretation for different aspects of the symbols evolved. The most significant systems of interpretation were associated with two major ways of thought: Confucianism and Taoism. The religious experience of the Chinese eventually unified aspects of both these traditions, along with others of Buddhist origin. However, in ancient times, these philosophies represented vastly different perspectives on the world, with opposing political implications. And while the concept that Tao underlies the interaction of Yin and Yang held great importance for Confucianists and Taoists alike, each understood and professed it in somewhat different ways.

The Taoists considered themselves experts on Tao, concerned especially with coming to know it. However, it must be acknowledged that Confucianists were also esteemed in matters concerning Tao: "The Great Treatise" of the *I Ching* is, after all, a Confucianist document, containing many sayings attributed to Confucius himself. Furthermore, Tao is often mentioned in other classic writings of Confucianism. In the *Analects* of Confucius, Tao is applied to a state

of social order entailing good government and proper rule of law. For
example:

> The Master said, "When Tao prevails in a state, one may be strong
> and bold in language as well as action. When Tao does not prevail,
> one may be strong and bold in action but must speak with
> reserve."[8]

In some passages, more specific references to the proper governance
under the rule of the emperor are cited:

> Confucius said, "When Tao prevails in the empire, ceremonies,
> music, and the chastisement of wrongdoers proceed from the
> emperor. When Tao does not prevail in the empire, ceremonies,
> music, and the chastisement of wrongdoers proceed from the local
> dukes."[9]

Such references in the *Analects* reveal how the Confucianist took Tao
seriously as a component of life—even at the political level.

But the Confucianist interpretation of Tao is not reserved to
proper conduct among powerful rulers. The grandson of Confucius,
Tze Tzu, is credited with having written the *Chung Yung* (Doctrine of
the Mean), wherein Tao pertains to simple and fundamental
relationships among ordinary people in everyday life. The *Chung
Yung* emphasizes that in order to be in harmony with Tao, it is
necessary constantly to guide one's spirit and discipline one's nature.
Its first chapter states:

> To guide one's nature is the Tao [path]. To nurture this Tao is
> called education [or religion]. The Tao must not be left, even for a
> moment. What is left at any moment is not the Tao.[10]

This typifies the Confucianist tendency to conceive of Tao as a moral
ideal which becomes embodied in men—both as individuals and as
members of society—through moral instruction.

In some Confucianist writings, the word "Tao" even has Utopian
connotations. This interpretation asserts an ideal of universal order
and unselfishness that has never been actualized, perhaps, except in
some distant past. The *Li Chi* (Book of Ritual), considered, with the *I
Ching* and *Shu Ching*, among the five "bibles" of Confucianism,
illustrates this ideal/Tao principle in the famous passage below:

> When the great Tao prevailed, the whole world was one Community. Men of talents and virtue were chosen [to lead the people]; their words were sincere and they cultivated harmony. Men treated the parents of others as their own, and cherished the children of others as their own. Competent provision was made for the aged until their death; work for the able-bodied; education for the young .... But now the Great Tao is disused and eclipsed. The world [the empire] has become a family inheritance. Men love only their own parents and their own children. Valuable things and labor are used only for private advantage....[11]

There can be little question but what the Confucianist tradition interpreted Tao to promote social responsibility and commitment to highest human standards.

The Taoist tradition interpreted the significance of Tao from a different perspective, although there are points of similarity. Lao Tzu, author of *Tao Te Ching*, is thought to have been a contemporary of Confucius (6th century B.C.). But this ancient classic—and the *Chuang Tzu*, written about two centuries later—develop the idea of Tao along a non-Confucianist line. Like "The Great Treatise" of the *I Ching*, these writings regard Tao in a cosmological context. However, they do not speak of Tao in terms of moral rectitude and orderly government. A particularly succinct illustration from the twenty-fifth chapter of the *Tao Te Ching* reads:

> There is something evolved from chaos, which existed before heaven and earth. It is inaudible, does not depend on anything, never changes. It pervades everything at all times. It may be thought of as the mother of all things under heaven. We do not know an appropriate name for it, so we give it the name "Tao"....[12]

Here, as in the *I Ching*, the Tao is represented as a formless reality underlying the entire universe. Bereft of perceivable characteristics and beyond the processes of change that affect all things, Tao nevertheless is regarded as the ultimate source of all things. Significantly, as originator of the universe, Tao is identified with the female role of "mother." As we shall see, the female aspect of Tao is of great importance to Taoists.

The above passage recalls the dilemma with which we began our study of Tao. So primal is this entity that it might be called "being" or "essence." It emanates from all things in the cosmos, but it is more than any one noumenal experience. Chapter 21 of the *Tao Te Ching* elaborates:

> The Tao is indistinct and intangible. But though indistinct and intangible, within it there are images. Though intangible and indistinct, within it there are objects. . . . It has existed from the earliest time; only its name is recent. It is the primary origin of all things.[13]

Like the Confucianist tradition, then, this interpretation sees Tao as a fundamental and precious entity that is the substance and the spirit of all experience. But no moral restrictions govern the validity of this Tao. It is its own existence.

This said, it would be incorrect to suppose that Lao Tzu's concept of Tao is limited to cosmological speculation. Chapter 46 of the *Tao Te Ching* conveys an example of Tao's moral and political implications as well:

> When Tao prevails in the world, horses are employed to work the farm. When Tao does not prevail in the world, horses are bred on the outskirts of the city for use in war.[14]

Lao Tzu echoes the sentiments of Confucius by characterizing an orderly society as a meaning or manifestation of Tao. But here the point must be made that Tao is equated with a state of peace and, by inference, is essential to the sustaining of that state. Although the Confucianist detested warfare, he would consider war necessary in certain circumstances. According to such thinking, Tao prevails not as a deterrent to war but as assurance that military campaigns will be organized and conducted only by the emperor, not by local strongmen who have no respect for law.

The philosophy developed in *The Writings of Chuang Tzu* is generally consistent with that of Lao Tzu. Chuang Tzu's notion of Tao corresponds to that expressed in the *Tao Te Ching*, but in a less austere writing style. Compare the excerpt below to the teachings we have already sampled:

Tung-kuo Tzu [T]: Where is the Tao that you are always talking about?
Chuang Tzu [C]: Everywhere.
T: If you could give me an example, it might seem more plausible.
C: The Tao is in this ant.
T: How about lower things?
C: The Tao is in weeds.
T: And in things even lower than that?
C: The Tao is in earthen-ware tiles.
T: Even lower?
C: The Tao is in dung.
Tung-kuo Tzu asked no further questions.[15]

While emphasizing the all-pervasiveness of Tao, Chuang Tzu tends to avoid speaking of it as a moral ideal, an aspect disputed by the Confucianist. The above dialogue advances only the universality of Tao and a disregard for conventional human biases.

Indeed, there are passages in his writing which imbue Tao with an amoral nature. Confucianists to the contrary, this Taoist view of the Tao principle asserts that moral rectitude is not a condition of Tao. At least, it indicates that Tao exists in evil as well as in goodness. In Chapter 10 of his writings, Chuang Tzu recounts the story of a notorious robber named Chih. When asked by one of his followers whether there is Tao in the activities of a robber, Chih replies:

What profession is there which has not its Tao? That the robber in his recklessness comes to the conclusion that there are valuables in a building shows his sagacity; that he is first to enter it shows his bravery; that he is last to leave it shows his righteousness; that he knows whether [the robbery] should be attempted shows his intelligence; and that he makes an equal division of the plunder shows his benevolence. Without all these five qualities, no one has ever become a great robber.[16]

Thus does Chuang Tzu find positive attributes even in a petty criminal. The ends to which these attributes are directed, according to Chih at least, cannot be governed by the ethics of the emperor. Tao exists in the thug as surely as it exists in the weeds and dung.

Actually, the writings of Lao Tzu and Chuang Tzu in themselves give only a glimpse of the Taoist understanding of the Tao. In order

to appreciate it more fully, we must go beyond the words with which
the ancient sages explained their views. It is the practices and customs
developed by Taoists through the centuries in which their understanding of Tao was embodied. According to traditional Taoist
history, these practices existed hundreds of years before the concept
was ever recorded in the classics. A key figure in the development of
these practices—although by no means their originator—was
Hwang Ti, the so-called Yellow Emperor, who ruled China from 2697
to 2597 B.C.

In Book 11 of the *Chuang Tzu*, it is reported that in the
nineteenth year of his reign, Hwang Ti journeyed to K'ung-tung
Mountain in order to visit the immortal sage Kuang Ch'eng Tzu and
ask him about the essential nature of Tao. According to this
account,[17] Hwang Ti at first had difficulty getting the master to
answer his questions. But when he succeeded, Hwang Ti was able to
apply his newfound understanding of Tao to several worldly sciences.
It is said that his fundamental discoveries later influenced the
development of military strategy, medical science and health practices, and the principles of meditation.

Traditional belief has it that after successfully ruling the empire
for a full hundred years, Hwang Ti rode off into heaven on the back
of a dragon and became one of the immortals. Chinese scholars of the
Confucianist tradition have long doubted Chuang Tzu's account and
tend to be skeptical about the premise that Tao practices are so
ancient in origin. Yet it is unlikely that the stories of Hwang Ti are
completely groundless, for even "The Great Treatise" of the *I Ching*
mentions him as a great emperor and describes many of his
accomplishments.[18]

In like fashion, another commonly heard claim is that Lao Tzu,
too, was merely a character of legend, a product of Taoist
imagination whose function it was to provide the settings for the
teachings of Taoists. Actual events from such ancient times are
indeed difficult to document, but there may be sound explanations
for these charges. We must keep in mind that such doubts may have
been kept alive due to Confucianist bias concerning official historical
accounts. It is, in fact, remarkable that the life of Lao Tzu is known
to us at all, for his writings clearly express a preference for
anonymity.

In any case, the influence of these great teachers is undeniable, for it has long been a common practice of Chinese writers to use the term "Hwang-Lao" when referring to Taoist principles and techniques. Formed by contracting the names of Hwang Ti and Lao Tzu, the name reflects the esteem with which both are regarded as ancestors of Taoism.

In the chapters that follow, several aspects of Taoism, its principles, and its practices will be described. It will be seen that in the civilization of China, Tao has been manifest in popular religious and political movements. We shall further trace its evolution and use of techniques as they apply to the growth of technology and the style of everyday living. Our discussion will be organized around a definite historical framework, but only as one component in a broader Taoist view of the world. The present book reflects a desire to communicate to the Western reader an authentic Taoist understanding of Tao and its significance, based on first-hand experience.

NOTES

1. *Tao Te Ching*, ch. 1; see Chang Chung-yuan, *Tao: A New Way of Thinking*, New York: Harper and Row, 1975, p.1.

2. See chs. 21 and 25, for example.

3. *Tao Te Ching*, ch. 1; see Arthur Waley, *The Way and Its Power*, New York: Grove Press, 1958, p. 141.

4. *Ta Chuan*, ch. 5, p. 3; see *The I Ching or Book of Changes*, trans. Richard Wilhelm and Cary F. Baynes, Princeton University Press, 1967, p. 298 (hereafter cited as Wilhelm/Baynes).

5. *Shu Ching*, book 2, p. 61; see *The Chinese Classics (CC)* trans. James Legge, Hong Kong University Press, 1960, vol. 3, p. 61.

6. *Ta Chuan*, ch. 5, p. 1; see Wilhelm/Baynes, *op. cit.*, p. 297.

7. *Ta Chuan*, ch. 10, p. 1; see Wilhelm/Baynes, *op. cit.*, p. 351.

8. *Analects*, book 14, ch. 4; see *CC*, vol. 1, p. 276.

9. *Analects*, book 16, ch. 2; see *CC*, vol. 1, p. 310.

10. Chung Yung, ch. 1, pp. 1-2; see *CC*, vol. 1, pp. 383-84.

11. *Li Yuen*, ch. 9; translation quoted directly from Joseph Needham, *Science and Civilization in China*, Cambridge University Press, vol. 2 (1956), p. 167.

12. See *The Texts of Taoism, (TT)*, trans. James Legge, Oxford University Press, 1891, part 1, p. 67. See also Waley, *op. cit.*, p. 174.

13. See Chang Chung-yuan, *op. cit.*, p. 55; and *TT*, pt. 1, p. 64.

14. See Chang Chung-yuan, *op. cit.*, p. 117, and Waley, *op. cit.*, p. 199.

15. *The Writings of Chuang Tzu*, book 22; see *TT*, part 2, p. 66.

16. Quoted from *TT*, part 1, pp. 283-85.

17. See *TT*, part 1, pp. 297-300.

18. *Ta Chuan*, part 2, ch. 2; see Wilhelm/Baynes, *op. cit.*, pp. 331-35.

CHAPTER 2
ANCIENT TAOIST HERMITS

Like Tao itself, Taoism has many aspects and is rather difficult to define precisely. As is it manifest in traditional Chinese culture, it has a deeply religious character; but, rather than being identified by a fixed set of beliefs and formal rituals, it has evolved as a loosely organized combination of ideas, practices, and customs. Those who have regarded themselves as Taoists have not always meant the same things by this word, while some who have not called themselves Taoists have nevertheless followed Taoist principles and practices in their ways of living.

The terms Tao Chia and Tao Chiao both may be understood to refer to Taoists, but each implies a distinctly different approach to the concept. The former term connotes a philosophical perspective, based on the ancient writings of Lao Tzu, Chuang Tzu, and the like; the latter refers to religious sects, organized during and after the second century A.D., whose practices often differ from those implied in the classic teachings. While both use meditation and alchemy, Tao Chiao relies more on superstition and formal ritual than the earlier practices of independent, asocial Tao Chia.

These earliest Taoists often led solitary lives in remote reaches of China, dedicating themselves to the values of individualism, personal freedom, and harmony with the processes of nature. This lifestyle is aptly summarized in the following anonymous Chinese folk song:

When the sun rises, I go to work;
When the sun sets, I rest.
I dig a well for my drink;
I plow the fields for my food.
The power of the ruler cannot influence me;
I follow the rule of nature.

The first two lines describe the daily routine of activity and rest, determined entirely by natural processes. The third and fourth indicate that all things needed for life—even those most necessary to survival—are acquired through the individual's direct interaction with the land, without reliance on others. The final lines profess the superiority of natural laws over the arbitrary and transient power of men and society.

Preferring obscurity, most Tao Chia hermits have long since been forgotten. Nevertheless, in their time, a number of them were respected as great sages and excelled as scholars. Prestigious government posts were offered to the most renowned of them, but the hermits rejected such promises of fame and politcal power with easy disdain. *The Writings of Chuang Tzu* is among the many Chinese historical sources relating the example of Hsu Yu, who was held in such esteem that the Emperor Yao (2357–2257 B.C.) volunteered to abdicate the throne in his favor. The sage refused.[1] According to legend, immediately after he refused, he went down to the river and washed his ears. After a while, a boy came along bringing a team of oxen to the river for a drink. Noticing Hsu Yu, he approached him and asked, "Why are you washing your ears again and again?" Hsu Yu answered, "Emperor Yao has just told me he wants to give up his throne and make me the emperor. After hearing his words, my ears feel so dirty I have to keep washing them out." When the boy heard this he immediately became alarmed and drove his oxen out of the water. Hsu Yu asked him, "Why are you taking your animals away from the river? They have not finished their drink and are still thirsty." The boy replied, "The filth from your ears is dirtying the river water. Do you think I want all that dirty water in my oxen's mouths?"

The sense of revulsion at the thought of political involvement is felt not only by the Taoist sage but also by the unsophisticated peasant boy who can have only the vaguest idea of Taoist philosophy. This illustrates how the undercurrent of disdain for politics and opposition to government power pervades Chinese thought and is felt by many people who cannot be considered Taoists in any official sense.

Ancient accounts of reclusive farmers who withdrew from society and protested against government are to be found not only in the Taoist writings, but even in the classics of the Confucianist school. The Confucian *Analects* tells of two occasions on which Tze-lu, a student of Confucius, met such characters while accompanying the Master, who often journeyed from one state to another, attempting to convince the rulers of the rightness of his political ideas. On one occasion, as Confucius and Tze-lu rode through the countryside in a carriage, they passed by Chang Tzu and Chieh Ni, who were working in a field. Tze-lu was sent to inquire of them where to ford a nearby river. When Chieh Ni found out that the driver of the carriage was Confucius, he asked Tze-lu: "Rather than following someone who merely withdraws from this state and then that one, would it not be better to follow those who have withdrawn from the world altogether?" Having said this, he went on with his farm work.²

On another occasion, Tze-lu fell some distance behind as he accompanied the Master on foot. After a while, he met an old man carrying a weed basket, and asked him, "Have you seen my Master?" The old man replied, "Your four limbs are unaccustomed to labor; you are unfamiliar with the five kinds of grain—who is your Master?" With that, he went on weeding.³

The values of such people are described more explicitly in certain passages in the writings of Meng Tzu (Mencius), the greatest sage of Confucianism after Confucius. Meng Tzu, who lived during the fourth century B.C., tells of two farmers who visited the state of T'eng, where Meng Tzu was advising the ruler on how to govern the people in a benevolent manner. One of them, Hsu Hsing, had come from Chou state. The other, Ch'en Hsiang, had arrived somewhat more recently from Sung state. The latter had a chance to meet Meng Tzu and told him what he had found out from Hsu Hsing:

The ruler of T'eng is a good ruler but he has not learned of the Tao. A ruler who knows the Tao works on the farm with the people. He prepares his own breakfast and supper, and at the same time reigns over the government. But the ruler of T'eng has his granaries, treasuries, and arsenals, the results of oppressing the people in order to feed himself. How can he be considered a good ruler?[4]

Although the Confucianist writings do not refer to these reclusive farmers as Taoists, the philosophy of Taoism—which received its highest expression in the classics of Lao Tzu and Chuang Tzu—was based essentially on the experiences and values of such people. Indeed, it is quite likely that the authors of the great Taoist classics were themselves characters of this kind.

According to the most reliable information about Lao Tzu, he spent many years as a low-level civil servant, curator of the royal library in Chou state. Finally, he went off into the high mountains to the west and became a hermit. It is said that as he traveled through the mountain pass at Han Ku Kuan, he was approached by the commander of the guards and customs officials stationed at the border there, a man named Hsi, who recognized him as a sage and requested him to write down a summary of his thought and experience. Lao Tzu complied with Hsi's request and gave him a manuscript containing some five thousand characters. This was the origin of the writings that later came to be known as the *Tao Te Ching*. In these writings, Lao Tzu put great emphasis on the value of solitude, quiescence, and humility; counseled inaction and lack of involvement with the ways of society; and criticized rulers who manipulate and interfere with the lives of the people. These themes are to be found again and again throughout the *Tao Te Ching*, and many illustrative passages could be quoted. Here are a few brief examples:

When a man is content to dwell in the most humble place, and when he always follows his true nature, he achieves natural simplicity.[5]

When one has attained the deepest humility and experienced extreme quietude, he can observe the natural cycle of changes in all living things.[6]

Abide by inaction. Do not strive for accomplishment. Discard learning. Consider large things the same as small, much and little as the same. Deal with what is easy as though it were difficult, with what is trivial as if it were important.[7]

While it is undeniable that the *Tao Te Ching* has great depth and subtlety and must be considered far more than a simple affirmation of the simple life of the hermit farmer, these and other passages are easy to understand if one keeps in mind that such a life was the ultimate choice of their author.

No less an example of such a life was that of Chuang Tzu, who lived about two centuries later than Lao Tzu, during a time when Chinese society was characterized by rapid cultural development as well as political controversy. Chuang Tzu was also employed for a time as a minor official, in charge of the attendants of the Ch'i Yuan gardens,* in Ch'u state, but he preferred to live in freedom and solitude, avoiding involvement with society. He became famous as a sage during his lifetime and had several opportunities to obtain positions of influence in the various states that were competing among themselves for territory and power, but he invariably refused them. On one occasion, he told two representatives of the king of Ch'u, who wanted him to become his prime minister, that he was like a tortoise who would rather keep dragging his tail in the mud than be killed so his shell could be honored in the king's ceremonies.[8]

According to another story, Chuang Tzu once went to visit his friend Hui Tzu, who was at that time minister of state in Liang. While he was on his journey, some gossip reported to Hui Tzu that Chuang Tzu was on his way to Liang to convince the king to appoint him to take over Hui Tzu's position. Hui Tzu became very worried. But when Chuang Tzu arrived three days later, he joked with his friend and said to him:

In the south there is a bird called a phoenix. During its migration flight, it stops to rest only on the branches of the dyandra tree, eats

*"Ch'i means lacquer; "yuan" means garden. It may be that Chuang Tzu was in charge of a district named for its lacquer trees—similar to such Western appellations as the Pine Tree State or Oak Ridge—rather than being the head of a single limited grounds area.

only the fruit of the bamboo, and drinks only the purest spring water. Once, while on its journey, it flew past an owl grasping a putrid rat it had just got. When the owl saw the phoenix, it gave an angry screech to frighten it away. Now do you, possessing the kingdom of Liang, wish to frighten me away with a similar screech?[9]

As is evident in this story, Chuang Tzu did not merely refuse political office, he regarded the prospect of political involvement with genuine distaste. A similar conclusion can be drawn from many other passages in his writings. In some of his most fascinating accounts, he goes beyond advocating a withdrawal from society to live a simple life on the farm and carries the ideals of inaction and indifference to extreme lengths. The following is his description of Tseng Tzu, a sage who lived in the state of Wei.

He wore a robe of woven hemp, and had no outer garment; his complexion was bad, and his hands and feet were horny and calloused. Sometimes he went for three days without building a fire. In ten years he never got new clothes; if he put his hat on straight its strings would break; his elbows had worn through his sleeves; and when he put on his shoes, the heels would break. Yet as he dragged his shoes along, he would sing a famous old song in a loud voice that sounded as if it came from a bell or sounding stone. The Emperor himself could not get him to be a minister, nor was he a friend of the feudal lords. What is to be learned from Tseng Tzu is that he who is nourishing his mind forgets about his body, that he who is nourishing his body forgets about all profit, that he who is carrying out the Tao forgets even his own mind.[10]

Here it is apparent that the Taoist philosophy of Chuang Tzu involves a thorough indifference to the conditions of life as well as the ways of society. Such a Taoist lives a completely aimless life, caring not a whit whether he is rich or poor. Indeed, he doesn't even care whether he lives or dies. He is a totally useless good-for-nothing who is content simply to let things happen as they may. Chuang Tzu was fond of pointing out the advantages of uselessness. Once, as he walked in the mountains, he came upon a very old tree with huge branches and luxuriant foliage. Seeing a woodchopper nearby, he asked why he did not chop it down and was told that its wood was useless. Later, taking some students to see it, he told them, "This tree, because its wood is good-for-nothing, will succeed in completing its natural life."[11]

Such a philosophy of life, with its emphasis on indifference, uselessness, and inaction makes an unlikely basis for social organization and action of a political or religious nature. Indeed, later Taoism, to the extent that it developed and emphasized such organized action, seems to have forgotten or neglected the original philosophy of the classics. Yet this philosophy continued to be influential in Chinese life and thought, inspiring many to drop out of official society and live aimlessly, often as recluses in the wilderness.

This influence is typified by the Seven Sages of the Bamboo Forest, a group of poets and wits who lived during the Chin dynasty (3rd and 4th centuries A.D.). Although they nominally held civil service positions, they led useless, dissolute lives, becoming drunk on wine every day, and spending almost all their time in idle talk or wandering about aimlessly. One of these sages, Liu Ling, about to go out after drinking all day, is said to have asked a servant to follow behind him with a shovel. "In case I die," he told the servant, "just bury me wherever I happen to drop."

A somewhat different example from a slightly later period is the story of T'ao Yuan Mein (c. A.D. 400), who was governor of a small territory known as Peng Tzei, in Kiangsi Province. He came to feel very tired of his life in society and disgusted by having continually to flatter the nobles and rich people and associate with politicians and bureaucrats. So he quit his job and retired to a farm in the country, saying, "I can no longer bow down for five bushels of rice." Later, he wrote a famous essay about his decision to retire, entitled *Kuei Ch'u Lai Tzu*, which means "Return to Home." In it he explained that he had gone home "because my farm and garden had become overgrown with weeds." He summed up his view of life as follows:

> To be rich and to have a high position is not my wish.
> Immortality cannot be expected.
> How long can I live in the world?
> Why don't I just free my mind and let time pass?

Even in retirement, however, T'ao Yuan Mein had definite ideas about social organization. These he explained in his *Tao Hwa Yuan Chi* (Record of Peach Blossom Park) in which he envisioned a utopian society where people live in small, peaceful groups, following old-fashioned customs and avoiding all contact with outsiders. This utopian ideal, which can also be found in the classics of Lao Tzu and Chuang Tzu, will be further discussed in a later chapter.

Although T'ao Yuan Mein was fond of wine, he apparently did not go in for the kind of habitual drunkenness that characterized the Seven Sages of the Bamboo Forest and many other Taoists. But it would be a mistake to regard their drunkenness as a perversion of Taoist principles. On the contrary, the kind of unconscious oblivion realized in a drunken stupor seems to be quite consistent with the life advocated by the ancient Taoists. Even in the *Chuang Tzu* there is a passage that describes the drunkard with what must be regarded as approval:

> Take the drunkard who falls from a cart. Though his bones and joints are like everybody else's, he suffers injuries differently from others because his spirit is intact. He knows nothing about the cart or the fall. He is unconcerned about life and death, so he is not afraid to collide with things. He is like this because of the integrity he has derived from wine.[12]

The approval is tempered, however, for the passage continues: "How much more efficient he would be if he derived his integrity from nature!"

The great poet of the T'ang dynasty, Li Po, whose work is well-known in Western translation, was one of the most famous drunkards in Chinese history. He drank wine all day long under all conditions. After he was already acclaimed as a great poet, the emperor T'ang Hsuan Tsung (A.D. 713–755) once invited him to his palace in order to meet him. Li Po arrived drunk, dressed in shabby and disheveled clothing, and explained to the emperor rather sheepishly, "I am the Immortal Drunkard." In one of his poems he compared himself to the madman of Ch'u (alluding to a character described in the *Analects* of Confucius, book 18), singing loudly and laughing at Confucius. Another poet of the T'ang period described him by saying, "A single quart of wine enables him to produce a hundred poems." Li Po finally died when he fell into the Yangtze river near Nanking while drunk, and attempted to embrace the moon reflected in the water. Though he did not officially call himself a Taoist, he was a true Taoist character.

NOTES

1. *Chuang Tzu*, book 1, see *The Texts of Taoism (TT)*, trans. James Legge, Oxford University Press, 1891, part 1, pp. 169–70.

2. *Analects*, book 18, ch. 6; see *The Chinese Classics (CC)*, trans. James Legge, Hong Kong University Press, 1960, vol.1, p. 333–34.

3. See *CC*, vol. 1, p. 335.

4. *Meng Tzu*, book 3, ch. 4; see *CC*, vol. 2, pp. 246–47 and also Needham, *Science and Civilization in China*, vol. 2, p. 120–21.

5. See *TT*, vol. 1, ch. 28, p. 71.

6. *Ibid.*, ch. 16, p. 59.

7. *Ibid.*, ch. 63, p. 106.

8. *Ibid.*, p. 390.

9. *Ibid.*, p. 391.

10. *Ibid.*, vol. 2, p. 158.

11. *Ibid.*, p. 27.

12. *Ibid.*, pp. 13–14.

chapter 3
taoist religion

The hermits who lived by Taoist principles and attitudes had no interest whatever in anything ordinarily regarded as characteristic of organized religion. Taoism, as they practiced it, was more a way of thought or philosophy of life than a religion.

During the Han dynasty, beginning in the second century A.D., a new kind of Taoism developed in China that had little in common with traditional Taoist philosophy. Among its main characteristics were belief in many gods and ghosts, the practice of magic spells and superstitious rituals, and an organization with a hierarchy of leadership. While traditional Taoism had been entirely a matter of individual belief, the new Taoism had an organizational structure similar to that of the government. It not only attempted to unite masses of people in support of Taoist leaders but ultimately engaged in political action.

The first religious and political organization of this kind was founded in A.D. 106 by Chang Tao Ling, an alchemist and magician whose family had long been interested in Taoist philosophy.* Chang

---

*One of his ancestors, five generations before him, was the famous Taoist military strategist Chiang Liang, discussed in Chapter 5.

Tao Ling was deeply influenced by the ideas of Mahayana Buddhism, which had been first brought to China by Indian missionaries in 305 B.C. and had gained widespread popularity by the first century A.D. Chang recognized the unique and powerful appeal to the Chinese people inherent in Buddhism: its complex and fanciful mythology of gods and goddesses, its elaborate rituals and magical practices. At the same time, he realized that this appeal did not depend on its specifically Buddhist aspects. With this in mind, he sought to create a religious movement of a similar character, but based on Taoist ideas and images. To do this, he invented a world of gods and goddesses resembling the Buddhist pantheon. While adopting other theories and practices similar to those of Buddhism, his new movement retained many tenets of traditional Taoism, including the symbolism of the *I Ching*. Among the gods worshiped as the original ancestors of the religion were Hwang Ti and Lao Tzu. In the case of Lao Tzu, scant attention was paid to the philosophy contained in his actual writings, but his name was often invoked in rituals and in casting magic spells.

With this amalgam of myth, philosophy, and superstition as a base, Chang Tao Ling soon established a remarkably successful religious organization. He evidently possessed considerable skill as a magician, for he went about working spectacular miracles, casting out devils, curing diseases, and the like, which attracted a great number of followers. And he knew how to reap the benefits of his success. Those who were cured or who became his followers after witnessing his magic were required to make a donation of five bushels of rice; thus, his organization soon became known as the "Five Bushels of Rice Religion." Before long, there were so many followers that the religion became a mass movement capable of wielding political power.

Eventually, Chang Tao Ling was able to establish a semi-independent state on the border between Szechwan and Shansi provinces. When he died, his position as religious and political leader was inherited by his descendants, first his son, Chang Heng, and then his grandson, Chang Lu. The political power of these leaders was somewhat lessened after A.D. 215, when Chang Lu submitted to the government of Wei, but his descendants continued to enjoy great respect and influence as religious prelates. In 1339, during the Yuan dynasty, they received the title T'ien Shih (Heavenly Teacher) and were recognized as the "popes" of Taoism. During and after the Ming dynasty they, like the descendants of Confucius, were supported by regular stipends, and held government positions considered equivalent in rank to vice-minister. The present Heavenly Teacher, Chang Erh Pu, lives on Taiwan, where he fled during the Communist revolution. Among the peasants in the countryside, he is still respected and feared as the ruler of ghosts and monsters.

The religion of Chang Tao Ling was only the first of many religious sects which evolved as a result of the Taoist response to Buddhism during and after the Han dynasty. The methods which led to Chang Tao Ling's success were also available to many other Taoist alchemists and magicians, and variants of his religion soon proliferated. After the third century, these cults became more elaborate and sophisticated, building temples in many places and creating a great body of religious writings, many of which imitated the Buddhist sutras.

This development must be understood in the context of the major growth in religious consciousness that occurred throughout Chinese society in the centuries following the disintegration of the Han dynasty. These centuries were a period of great turmoil and suffering in China. There were many secret wars and the constant threat of barbarian invasions. Political assassinations were frequent and sometimes involved the execution of entire families. The economy failed disastrously, and civilization fell into ruin. In this chaotic atmosphere, religions thrived 'and new religious ideas attracted many followers.

The most striking growth was to be seen in the popularity and influence of Buddhism. This was partly due to the increasing activity of Buddhist missionaries from India, who brought many writings and introduced new ideas and practices throughout the period. Among these was the monk Da Mo (Daruma), who came to China near the beginning of the sixth century and introduced Ch'an Buddhism, which the Japanese call "Zen." But it is likely that the real reasons behind the success of Buddhism in China had more to do with the peculiar attraction of the Buddhist viewpoint and attitude for the Chinese people during this long and troublesome period. With its emphasis on reincarnation, especially in the doctrine that a person's future rebirths would be influenced by his moral conduct in the present life, it seemed to offer hope for a better life in another world to those who bore their sufferings patiently. Moreover, it held out the promise that through a commitment to Buddhism one could obtain forgiveness for crimes and moral transgressions, thus avoiding the otherwise inevitable punishments after death. These ideas were attractive not only to the downtrodden peasants, but to officials and nobles as well. By the sixth century, its influence had even extended to the royal family, and the Emperor Liang Wu Ti (502–48) himself became a Buddhist monk.

The success of Buddhism had a powerful effect on the other traditions of thought, whose leaders felt great pressure to compete with the Buddhists for followers and influence. The Taoist cults put greater emphasis on the other-worldly aspects of their beliefs, and interpreted the ancient distinction between Yin and Yang in a new way, as representing the two different levels of reality: the world of men (Yang) and the world of ghosts (Yin). They also adopted more of the doctrines and practices of traditional Taoist philosophy in order to emphasize their distinctness from Buddhists. Among the literature produced as part of this development were many devotional writings, some regarded as having been divinely inspired, such as the *Ling Pao Ching* (Divine Precious Classic) supposedly revealed in a vision to Ko Hsuan, who also wrote the *Ch'ing Ching Ching* (Pure Calm Classic) and other books.

The T'ang dynasty (618–906) finally brought a long period of peace, prosperity and cultural renaissance to China. Indeed, like the Han dynasty, it represents a high point of civilization in which the Chinese nation realized some of its greatest achievements. During the nearly three centuries of its reign, the religious movements that had developed during the preceding period enjoyed prosperity and influence. It was early in this period that the Buddhist monk Hsuan Chwang (596–664) journeyed to India where he studied for years. When he returned to China in 645, he brought back many sutras and other texts, which he later translated from Sanskrit into Chinese. His journey became the basis of many legends which eventually culminated in the great novel *The Journey to the West (Hsi Yu Chi),* described in some detail in Chapter 11. But the development of

Buddhism was somewhat overshadowed during this period by that of Taoism, which attained a much greater level of respect and influence than it had previously known.

An important factor in this was the way in which Taoist religion became incorporated in the ancestor worship of the imperial family. The surname of the T'ang emperors was Li, the same as that of Lao Tzu. They believed they were his descendants, and thus the worship of Lao Tzu became an official practice. The Emperor Hsuan Tsung (713–755) was especially interested in Taoism and even wrote commentaries on the Taoist classics. He also nationalized the organization of the Taoist religion, dividing the whole empire into thirty-six districts, each having its own Taoist temple and hierarchy of officials similar to those of the government. (An analogous development in Western culture is perhaps the diocesan organization of the Roman Catholic Church.) As a result of this official importance and respect, Taoist scholarship, religious writing, and poetry flourished. Among the great Taoist authors of the period were the poet Li Po; Ssuma Ch'eng Cheng, who wrote the *T'ien Yin Tzu* (Book of the Heaven-Concealed Master) late in the seventh century; Li Ch'uan, the eighth-century author of *Yin Fu Ching* (Harmony of the Seen and the Unseen); and T'an Ch'iao, who wrote the *Hua Shu* (Book of Transformations) during the tenth century.

During the Sung dynasty Taoist religion continued to have official respect and influence. The Emperor Chen Tsung (998–1020) enlarged the already enormous Taoist pantheon and gave it a systematic organization modeled on that of the government bureaucracy, with complex hierarchies of officials. At the top were the *San Ch'ing* (Three Pure Ones), a trinity of supreme gods, which some have compared to the triune god of the Christian tradition: T'ien Pao, ruler of the past; Ling Pao (Jade Emperor), ruler of the present; and Shen Pao, ruler of the future. The Jade Emperor was probably regarded as the most powerful of these and was imagined as the heavenly counterpart of the emperor, ruling over all things and with nearly as many subjects. The vast literature of Taoist writings was also systematized during the Sung dynasty. An official library of works, the *Tao Tsang*, was collected and finally printed in 1190. It included documents from many periods, some very ancient, others, such as the *Yuen Chi Ch'i Ch'ien,* written as recently as Chen Tsung's time.

The Sung dynasty was eventually overthrown by invading Tartars from the north, first the Chi, who occupied Northern China and forced the imperial government to move south to Hangchow in 1126, and then the Yuan, who conquered the Southern Sung in 1279. During the ensuing period of foreign rule, Taoist religion underwent political change and began to have revolutionary aspects. Taoist sect organizations developed into centers of various kinds of anti-foreign and anti-government activity. Ironically, this represented in some ways a return to the political tendencies of the ancient Taoists. But the religious aspects of Taoism continued to evolve as well, and important new schools and branches were founded. During the Chin period in Shantung Province, near where the ancient state of Ch'i had been located, Wang Chung Yang and his disciples became known as the "Seven Enlightened Masters." One of these sages, Chiu-Ch'u Chi, later founded the Dragon Gate sect at Po Yuen Kuan (White Cloud Temple) in Peking. He was also invited to travel west with Genghis Khan; he later wrote an account of the travels of Hsuan Chwang, on which the famous Ming dynasty novel *The Journey to the West* was based. The Dragon Gate sect is still an active branch of Taoist religion on Taiwan.

The religion practiced by the Seven Enlightened Masters and their followers came to be known as the Northern School. Other sects were organized at about the same time under the Southern Sung, near the ancient territory of Ch'u state. An important leader was Po Yu Ch'an, also known as Ko Ch'ang Keng, one of the Five Southern Masters. He established the Southern School of Taoism and eventually was given the title Purple Pure and Bright Enlightened Master by the Emperor Sung Ning Tsung. Also during the Sung period, the T'ien Shih (Heavenly Teacher) sect moved south, establishing a temple on Dragon and Tiger Mountain in Kiangsi Province in 1016, which remained the principal center of this branch of Taoism until 1930. Another Taoist sect was the Mao San branch, founded by three brothers of the Mao family in Kiangsu Province, which became famous for its magic techniques.

chapter 4

taoists, confucianists, and buddhists

For centuries, the typical Chinese has experienced religion as a blend of attitudes and practices from three distinct traditions. Whereas two of these—Taoism and Confucianism—originated in ancient China, Buddhism arrived somewhat later from India. The ultimate aim for each of these religious philosophies has been the salvation of humanity through the deliberate control of conduct. The three differ greatly regarding the precise nature of salvation and the methods for attaining it. However, their underlying compatibility is manifest in the evolution of their relationships in Chinese history.

Actually, Taoism and Confucianism have a great deal in common. Both share a theoretical heritage, such as the symbolism of the *I Ching*. Beyond this, they follow common moral and philosophical presuppositions. In fact, they have influenced each other since quite early in their development. Considerable evidence suggests that Confucius himself met Lao Tzu and regarded him with great respect. Major differences do exist between the two traditions—as approaches to life and as teachings—but the nature of these differences is such that it is more accurate to think of them as complementary rather than conflicting. While the Taoist path of Lao Tzu is passive and inward, the teachings of Confucius are more actively extroverted in their ideal of virtue. When properly understood, the alleged disparity between these two approaches to human conduct do not compete with one another; indeed, they actually advance alternate sides of the same outlook on life and the universe. The richness of this combination can best be appreciated when we examine more closely the teachings and lives of their greatest sages: Confucius and Lao Tzu.

In the Confucian text of *The Great Learning*, the ancient way of virtue is described as follows:

> The ancients who wished to perpetrate great virtue throughout the empire first learned to govern their own states well. Wishing to govern their states well, they first put their family relationships in order. Wishing to have their families in order, they first cultivated their own lives. Wishing to cultivate their lives, they first regulated their minds.[1]

Confucius advocated a return to the ancient practices described here. It was his belief that the attainment of peace and prosperity throughout the world would ultimately be based on the virtue of the individual. Gradually, such conduct would accumulate into the majority until the reality produced by its actions would extend the rule of order and proportion to higher and higher levels of social organization.

As we saw in an earlier chapter, the Taoists envisioned a quite different path of virtue, withdrawing and isolating themselves, avoiding all interference with social affairs and competition with others. Yet in their own style, they also saw themselves as aiming at the realization of peace and prosperity throughout the world. The 80th chapter of the *Tao Te Ching* vividly describes utopia:

> The state should be small, and have only a few inhabitants. The ruler should teach the people to shun weapons even if they are available, to stay close to their homes and avoid travel. Thus though there might be ships and carriages, there would be no need to ride in them; and though there might be arms and weapons, there would be no need to use them. The ruler should also make the people return to the state of pure simplicity such as that which prevailed when only knotted cords were used [instead of writing]. Then they would enjoy the food they eat, consider the clothing

they wear suitable and regard their houses as comfortable, and enjoy their customs. The states might be so closely located that the barking of dogs and the crowing of roosters in one can be heard in the other. But the people in each would be content to live their entire lives at home, without traveling to visit their neighbors.

This passage is no less definite than many to be found in the Confucianist writings in its advocacy of universal peace and prosperity through orderly society. The difference is that Lao Tzu envisioned such a state as coming about not through social organization, which would balance and regulate conflicting interests. Instead, he advocated avoiding organization and returning to natural relationships and ways of living that he regarded as inherently peaceful and without competition. Thus the Taoist did not so much argue for an ethical and political system different from that of the Confucianists. He did not argue at all. Rather, he went off to mind his own business and believed that all would be well if everyone else did the same. The life of the average Chinese involved a certain amount of social commitment—including, for example, doing his civil service job well—but might also include gardening or solitary walks in the mountains. Thus he would not have to choose between Confucianism and Taoism, but could benefit from both.

Perhaps the best example of these differences (as well as the mutual compatibility) could be found in the relationship between Confucius and Lao Tzu. Confucius was a descendant of an aristocratic family. His father was an official in the territory of Tso, and he himself was minister of law and for a time acting premier of Lu. After he was forced to resign, he traveled extensively, associating and discussing moral and political ideas with rulers and statesmen throughout China. He had many students and followers, including several who later became famous themselves as teachers or as high officials in government. His life and activities were well known and preserved for posterity through accurate records kept by his followers. His teachings came to be admired by the emperors and were eventually established as the orthodox philosophy of China by the Han Emperor Wu Ti (140–97 B.C.). His descendants have been respected, given official positions, and supported by government stipends—even up to today on Taiwan.

The life of Lao Tzu, who was a somewhat older contemporary of Confucius', contrasts with this in virtually all respects. His origins are unknown. His minor civil service job was not a position of influence and did not bring him into much contact with others. After he retired, he became a hermit and had very few students. His travels and eventual whereabouts are obscure, subject merely to mysterious legends. His ideas were not of great benefit to the government and were never admired by the emperors. Although he was later worshiped as a god of the Taoist religion, this had nothing to do with the influence of his ideas, which were largely ignored by those who venerated him. Not many details about his life are known today. The biography we have is largely based on a few fragmentary pieces of information collected by the historian Ssuma Ch'ien (2d century B.C.). Yet a number of ancient sources indicate that Confucius visited Lao Tzu on one or more occasions and that their relationship was one of mutual respect and friendship. Such accounts are to be found in the *Chuang Tzu*, which includes a number of such stories (see ch. 14, "Movement of the Heavens"). They also appear in the family biography of Confucius, and in the Confucian classic of ritual, the *Li Chi*, in which a chapter entitled the "Questions of Tseng Tzu" mentions that Confucius consulted Lao Tzu on ritual matters.

The original relationship between the two masters gradually gave way to conflict and bickering among their students and followers, however. The early writers of the Confucianist school— such as Tze Sze, the grandson of Confucius who wrote the *Chung Yung* (Doctrine of the Mean)—show the favorable influence of Taoist ideas. But later, in the period of the Warring States, many Confucianists attacked and rejected Taoism. *The Writings of Meng Tzu* reflect some Taoist influence, such as in the development of the concept of *ch'i* ("spirit" or "breath"). However, this same source criticizes the social doctrines of Taoism as irresponsible and rejects the views of Mo Tzu, Yang Tzu, and others on the grounds that they fail to give due respect to the ancestral structure of the family.[2] On the other hand, the *Writings of Chuang Tzu*, a contemporary of Meng Tzu, contain many stories critical of the Confucianists and even portray Confucius himself as a foolish character.[3]

Taoism was never perceived as successfully competing against or offering a genuine political alternative to Confucianism. The influence of the Confucianists grew significantly during the Period of the Warring States. When the Han dynasty brought stability to China after the brief tyranny of the Ch'in, the ideas of Confucius came to be considered the official guidelines for the organization of society throughout the empire. In the meantime, the Taoists were withdrawing to the mountains and avoiding social influence. As a result, although they were not openly persecuted, many of the details of the early development of Taoism were forgotten or suppressed. The Confucianists refused to recognize the old stories of meetings between Confucius and Lao Tzu, especially those that made Confucius seem inferior by comparison. This led them to doubt many aspects of the Taoist historical accounts, calling into question whether Lao Tzu actually lived as long ago as the Taoists claimed, or even whether he actually existed. This skepticism had a long-term effect, since Confucianists dominated the field of historical research for centuries. It is among the reasons that so few historical facts are known today about Lao Tzu and other early Taoists.

After the first century A.D., when Buddhism became popular, the importance and prestige of Confucianism was not without challenge. As described in the last chapter, during the later Han and succeeding periods up to the T'ang dynasty, many Buddhist and Taoist religious cults flourished. Their influence spread throughout China, and even the emperors embraced them. Throughout these developments, the Confucianists found it necessary to fight to protect their own prestige and the Confucian heritage of the society against what they regarded as disorderly influences. They viewed the social changes brought about by the popularity of Buddhist and Taoist religions as causes of poverty and suffering for the people.

During the T'ang dynasty, a period of great Taoist influence, a scholar-statesman-poet named Han Yu (732–824) proved a particularly tough-minded spokesman for Confucianism. In his essay *Yuan Tao* (On the Origin of the Tao), he complained that the swelling number of religious functionaries was a drain on society's resources. "These days for every farmer who plows his field, there are six who want to eat," he said, "and when a craftsman makes his product, there are six who want to use it." He argued that the government should force the monks and Taoists to return to labor among the common people, that their temples should be used as common homes and their books burned, and that they should be re-educated "according to the Tao of the ancient kings."⁴ In another passage, he wrote: "If the emperor refuses to issue orders, he is not fulfilling his duty; if the officers refuse to assist the emperor in governing, they are not fulfilling their duty; if the people refuse to supply rice, grains, and silk, they should be executed."⁵ Ironically, Han Yu's own nephew was the famous Taoist sage Hen Shan Tzu, one of the so-called Pa Hsien (Eight Immortals).

Tough opposition to Buddhist and Taoist influence, such as Han Yu's, was not to prevail indefinitely, however. By two centuries later, a new synthesis was developing in Chinese religion. Sages and monks of all three traditions achieved unprecedented understanding and appreciation of the beliefs and actions of the others. Throughout the period of competition and dispute among religious sects, it was no doubt necessary for religious leaders and scholars to be well-informed about alternative points of view. In time, some came to be genuinely interested in them and adopted and practiced certain aspects of them. This tendency culminated in the new philosophical and religious movements that evolved during the Sung dynasty. Among these were Ch'an (Zen) Buddhism and also the philosophy known as neo-Confucianism.

The neo-Confucian philosophers developed a profound new interpretation of the Confucian classics as well as writings of Confucius that took into account much knowledge that was originally Taoist or Buddhist in origin. Thus their commentaries on *The Great Learning* and *The Doctrine of the Mean*, for example, show their awareness of the influence of the early Taoists upon certain aspects of those writings. Furthermore, their commentaries on the *I Ching* reveal their knowledge of traditional Taoist as well as Confucianist interpretations. They also adopted many Buddhist ideas. Tendencies in these directions were to some extent prefigured in the work of the Confucianist scholar Su Tung P'o, who was deeply influenced by his association with the Buddhist monk Fu Yin.

But the real flowering of neo-Confucianist thought took place later, in the eleventh century, when there were several remarkable philosophers, including Shao Yung (1011-77), Chou Tun Yi (1017-73), and the Ch'eng brothers: Hao (1032-85) and I (1033-1107).

Shao Yung was a mathematical prodigy as well as a great historian. He became most famous for his work on the *I Ching*, which included an intensive investigation of its cosmological implications as well as the invention of new techniques of using it for divination. His life was in some ways reminiscent of the ancient Taoist sages; for example, he refused many opportunities to become an official. The cyclic view of time, which is central to his theory of "Cosmological Chronology," shows the influence of Taoist and Buddhist ideas. Among his writings were the *Kuan Wu Phien* (Treatise on the Observation of Things) and the *Huang Chi Ching Shih Shu* (Book of the Sublime Principle).[6]

Chou Tun Yi was also a careful scholar who avoided positions of official prestige. He invented the famous diagram known as the *T'ai Chi Tu* and wrote a commentary explaining it. This diagram had several levels of meaning—some with cosmological importance, others pertaining to social relationships, human physiology, and other subjects as well. The philosophical basis of the diagram can be found in the *I Ching* and *The Doctrine of the Mean*, but it also contains many ideas of Taoist origin. Chou Tun Yi may also have been influenced by a similar but different diagram, invented by the T'ang dynasty Taoist sage Chen Tu'an, which represented the process of Taoist meditation.[7]

Among Chou Tun Yi's students were the Ch'eng brothers, both of whom became distinguished as philosophers, writers, and teachers. They were honest Confucians, but their writings show considerable Taoist influence, especially in their edition and commentary on *The Doctrine of the Mean*. The following poem by Ch'eng Hao typifies their understanding of classic Taoist ideas:[8]

Near the middle of the day, when clouds are thin and the breeze is light,
I stroll along the river, passing willows and blooming trees.
People of the day do not understand my joy;
They will say that I am loafing like an idle young man.

The Ch'eng brothers were also important as a result of their influence on Chu Hsi (1131-1200), who, though he lived two generations later, referred to "my master, the philosopher Ch'eng" in his commentaries on both *The Great Learning* and *The Doctrine of the Mean*.[9] Chu Hsi brought neo-Confucian thought to its most mature development and accomplished a great synthesis of the ideas of his predecessors. His articulation of the principles of Confucianism came to be considered authentic and has been accepted as orthodox even down to the present century. His commentaries on the ancient classics were regarded with nearly as much esteem as the ancient texts themselves. He became known as the "Third Sage of Confucianism," signifying that he surpassed all save Confucius himself and Meng Tzu in his knowledge of its teachings. Early in life, Chu Hsi was interested in the study of Taoism and Buddhism. Though he also passed the rigorous examination on the Confucianist classics at an early age, he did not declare his allegiance to Confucianism until he was nearly thirty, and it is said that this gesture was motivated by a desire to qualify for a better official position. Taoist and Buddhist ideas can be found throughout his many important writings, whose quality and prestige greatly contributed to the ultimate synthesis of the three religions of China.

The coming of Buddhism to China during the Han dynasty and its effect on the development of Taoist religion has been described in the previous chapter. As social movements, Buddhism and Taoism were quite similar. Those who became followers tended to retreat from society and concentrate on ritual ceremonies and other devotional practices. Centers of their activities were temples and monasteries: Taoist *Kuan* and Buddhist *Szu*. Some of them were very large, often located in remote mountainous areas. These exemplified complex forms of social organization—involving at some temples as many as a thousand people—and also wielded considerable economic power. It is on this level that the competition between Buddhism and Taoism can be most clearly understood, for on a deeper ideological level the relationship is more accurately regarded as imitation than as competition. The wealth (and ultimately the survival) of temples depended largely on the contributions of those who visited them and became their followers. At times, the competition for followers provoked some attacks. For example, during the fifth century, Southern China was ruled by Emperor Liang Wu Ti, who converted to Buddhism, and the Wei emperors in the north also respected the Buddhists. The Taoist Heavenly Teacher K'ou Ch'ien Tzu persuaded Emperor Wu Ti to become much more favorable toward the Taoists, and even to persecute the Buddhists. As a result, many Buddhist temples were destroyed. But before long, K'ou Ch'ien Tzu suffered a political reversal, falling so out of favor that he was executed, and the Wei emperor preferred Buddhism once again.

One of the "Five Eternal Prohibitions" of the Buddhist religion forbids the consumption of alcohol. Before this religion reached China, Confucianists and Taoists were not opposed to the drinking of wine. Therefore, when Buddhism began to win over many Chinese followers, this prohibition caused some problems. A large number of Chinese converts decided to select aspects of all three religions and ignore what did not suit them.

A case in point can be found in the essays of Po Ch'ü-i Shiang Shan (Chü Shih*) a statesman, poet, and writer of the T'ang dynasty. In one article, he describes the life of a character named "the drunk old poet," modeled in large part on himself. "The drunk old poet" served his whole life in dedication to public service in the government, culminating in the prestigious post of minister of justice. While such conduct was in keeping with Confucianist precepts, he had formally adopted the main teachings of Buddhism. However, his daily activities were more Taoist in the tolerance of drinking wine. In fact, he would get drunk early in the day and then, while soused, write poems as they occurred to him. Even as he wrote, he would continue to tipple—succumbing at last to a stuporous slumber. Though still drunk when he came to, he would reach for his pen to write more poems and, of course, resume his drinking. His wife observed that whenever he traveled, he took along two jugs of wine to partake from as he walked. When she could no longer abide his excesses, she reprimanded him severely, reminding him of his profession of Buddhism. "The old drunk poet" explained to his wife that drinking was a habit that resisted change, then added, "It may be a vice, but if I

*Chü Shih means "layman practicing Buddhism at home."

didn't drink I might indulge some even worse pastime!" Such reasoning was common among those who combined the philosophies of Taoism, Confucianism, and Buddhism in their practical lives.

This attitude of combining doctrines persisted in the centuries that followed. We know for instance, that during the North Sung dynasty (A.D. 960–1126), Su Shih acquired great fame as a government official in the Confucianist tradition. His poetry and prose pieces concerning Buddhist teachings also gained favor, under the pen-name Tung P'o Chü Shih. But Su Shih also indulged the drinking of wine—and the company of concubines—with the clear conscience of a Taoist.

By the time of the South Sung dynasty (A.D. 1127–1279), official government censures forbade the practice of Taoism and Buddhism as formal religions, although their study on an informal basis met with somewhat more tolerance. One such student at this time was Chu Hsi, whose father counseled him to adopt Confucianism in order to advance himself politically. Of all the written commentaries on Confucianist writings, Chu Hsi's were considered so outstanding that they became the official texts in schools throughout China.

During the Ming dynasty (1368–1644), Lee Chao En proposed that Buddhism, Taoism, and Confucianism be merged into one philosophical entity: Ta Ch'eng Chiao ("Great Success" religion) or Ta Hsueh Chiao ("Great Learning" religion), relying heavily on the influence of Confucianist teachings. By the time of the Ch'ing dynasty (1649–1911), his idea had grown so popular that ten thousand followers are estimated to have practiced it. Under such powerful religious leaders as Lee K'uang Hsin, celebrants in the northern part of Kiang-Su province convened every month in the mountains to read aloud the *Ta Hsueh* ("Great Learning"). Their solidarity and size were considered a threat to the government, who dispatched soldiers to suppress them. The slaughter of so large a religious faction reveals how far the merging of these doctrines had advanced since the time of Lee Chao En's proposal.

Such widespread and extreme conflict between these religious groups was unusual, however. For the most part, their competition was relatively peaceful, though it certainly had political implications. As we saw in the previous chapter, the T'ang dynasty emperors tended to favor the Taoists. One of them, T'ang Hsuan Tsung (713–55), was even a serious scholar and writer of Taoist literature. Yet others were quite interested in Buddhism, notably T'ang T'ai Tsung (627–45), who was Hsuan Tsung's great grandfather, and T'ang Hsian Tsung (806–14), Hsuan Tsung's great-great grandson. The possibility of changes in the popularity and influence of these religions indicates that both traditions had become deeply entrenched in Chinese life and culture. After the syntheses of the Sung dynasty, they were recognized as equal components of Chinese religion, along with Confucianism. By the time of the Ming dynasty, the assimilation of all three traditions was so complete that Lao Tzu, Confucius, and the Buddha could be pictured seated together in religious art. In more recent times, Chinese religion also assimilated aspects of other religious traditions—such as Christianity, Mohammedanism, and Zoroastrianism (now no longer practiced but influential during the T'ang dynasty).

A remarkable thing about religion in Chinese culture is that conflicts among religious sects have never led to major wars or mass killing. There is nothing in Chinese history to compare with the wars between the Christian crusaders and Moslems or those throughout Europe following the Christian Reformation. Though ideological conflicts have also had political and economic aspects, competing groups tended to accept one another's existence; and for the most part, neighboring temples and monasteries were on friendly terms.

NOTES

1. *The Chinese Classics (CC)*, trans. James Legge, vol. 1, Hong Kong University Press, 1960.

2. *Meng Tzu*, book 3, *CC*, vol. 2, p. 282.

3. See, for example, ch. 29 ("Robber Chih") and ch. 31 ("A Fisherman").

4. No author cited, *Collection of T'ang Dynasty Texts*, Taipei, Taiwan: Chi Wen Publications, no copyright or page numbers.

5. *Ibid.*

6. Joseph Needham, *Science and Civilization in China*, vol. 2, Cambridge University Press, 1956, pp. 595, 598.

7. Fung Yu-Lan, *A History of Chinese Philosophy,* trans. Derk Bodde, Princeton: Princeton University Press, 1953, pp. 434-51.

8. From Chang Chung-yuan, *Creativity and Taoism,* New York: Harper and Row, 1970, p. 170.

9. *CC,* vol. 1, pp. 355 and 382.

CHAPTER 5

TAOISM AND MILITARY STRATEGY

An important area in which the ideas of Taoist philosophy have found application throughout Chinese history is that of military strategy. Perhaps this seems unlikely in view of what we have described of Taoism in the earlier chapters. We have characterized the early Taoists as hermits and independent farmers who avoided contact with society and who seemed to think that all people would naturally get along peacefully if they were simply left alone, free of the coercion of government and other types of social organization. What could such a view of the world have to offer on ways to achieve success in war, the most aggressive, violent form of human interaction? The answer can be found in the classic Taoist writings, which develop an original and remarkably wise way of dealing with the problems and dangers of military confrontation, an approach that follows naturally from basic Taoist principles.

There are many passages in the *Tao Te Ching* that strongly condemn war and its evil consequences. For example, in Chapter 31 it is written:

> The weapons of war are implements of disaster, and should not be used unless it is unavoidable...war should be regarded as an occasion for mourning. When many people are killed, bitter grief should be expressed. Even the victor in battle should lament it.

But though his dislike of war is obvious, Lao Tzu clearly recognizes that there are circumstances that arise in which military confrontation cannot be avoided. Even those who wish to keep to themselves and avoid society may be forced to participate if their home territories are invaded or they are oppressed by cruel tyrants. To survive under such circumstances it is necessary to recognize the unusual nature of wartime conditions and be prepared to use extraordinary strategic means to achieve success. "Kingdoms can only be governed if rules are kept," wrote Lao Tzu, "but battles can only be won if rules are broken."[1] Lao Tzu's concept of military strategy is based on the idea that the defensive side has a great advantage in any confrontation and that it is possible for a comparatively weak force to defeat an attacker of far greater strength, provided it knows how to retreat skillfully and how to employ tricky and unexpected methods with decisive effect. Thus in Chapter 69 of the *Tao Te Ching*, an "ancient strategist" is quoted with approval:

> I do not venture to fight an offensive war. I prefer to be on the defensive. I would rather retreat a foot than advance an inch.[2]

And in Chapter 43 the philosophy of retreat is stated:

> The softest thing in the world can overcome the hardest. Such a thing seems to come from nowhere, yet it penetrates everywhere.[3]

Putting this kind of strategic concept into successful practice depends on preparation. One must become as well informed as possible about the enemy's condition and alternate courses of action. Above all, one must not underestimate his strength and be caught without the ability to react effectively. Thus Chapter 69 continues:

> Nothing can be more disastrous than engaging in war without being serious. To do so is to lose what is precious [the principle of Tao]. Thus in war, those who regard it as lamentable but necessary will win.

The reference to "what is precious" also refers to the so-called three precious things described in Chapter 67—the moral virtues most essential for success as a military commander. These are "compassion," "frugality," and "not-wanting-to-be-superior." The importance of the latter two is obvious. If one is not frugal in expending energy, material supplies, and soldiers' lives, one may not have the resources to accomplish decisive action at the proper time. And in order to maintain the defensive position without becoming discouraged, one must not be too anxious to dominate or prove one's superiority to the enemy. But compassion is also central to the Taoist attitude toward war, and Lao Tzu suggests that it is the key to the strategist's success:

> If one has compassion, he is sure to be victorious in battle and well protected in self-defense. Heaven will save such a man because of his compassion.

What compassion means in practical terms can be appreciated by considering the various aspects of the commander's job. First, he must be compassionate in dealing with his own troops. He will be a far more inspiring and effective leader if he shows kindness and appreciates the dangers and hardships of their situation than if he is insensitive and cruel. Second, he must be compassionate in dealing with the civilian population living in areas affected by his army's activities. If he is kind toward them and able to prevent his troops from looting or destroying their homes, they will support him, and their aid may be invaluable. Finally, he must be compassionate toward the enemy. This does not mean he should be reluctant to damage them when conditions are right. Rather, it is a matter of maintaining a certain attitude which keeps the fighting in its proper perspective. Lao Tzu expresses it as follows in Chapter 30:

> A skillful general strikes a decisive blow and then stops. He does not try to assert his mastery. He strikes the blow but does not take pride in it or boast about it. He strikes it as a matter of necessity, not from a desire for mastery.[4]

A strategy based on the philosophy of Lao Tzu is unsuitable if one's objective is to conquer others, but it is particularly effective if one is defending one's home against an invading force. There have been many occasions in history when Taoist groups have applied this philosophy in organizing rebellion and resistance against oppressive governments in the Chinese countryside. In comparatively recent times, theories of guerrilla warfare are ultimately based on Taoist principles.

In addition to its philosophical concepts, Taoism has developed a number of specific techniques that have had practical influence on the conduct of warfare in Chinese history. One example concerns the prediction methods based on the *I Ching,* involving the ideas of Yin and Yang, the eight trigrams and sixty-four hexagrams, and the five elements. Such methods have been used for purposes of military intelligence and planning since ancient times, and even in the twentieth century, Chinese and Japanese generals relied on information gotten in this way. And while such prediction methods were developed not only by the Taoists, the Taoist contribution was very significant. Another example concerns the development of techniques of martial arts, including methods of hand-to-hand combat and sword-fighting, which evolved from Taoist meditation practices. These will be described in a later chapter.

According to traditional Chinese history, the application of Taoist principles in military affairs goes back as far as the 26th century B.C. when the great emperor Hwang Ti used strategy to defeat the armies of the powerful invader Ch'ih Yu. It is said that Ch'ih Yu assembled a great force south of the Yangtze River, hoping to entice the emperor to engage in a battle in which he knew the imperial army would be crushed. Not only were Ch'ih Yu's armies superior in numbers to those of Hwang Ti, but they were far better equipped, with metal weapons, armor, and helmets vastly superior to the stone weapons and primitive protective garments available to the emperor's men. But Hwang Ti did not rush to join battle; instead, he retreated to the mountainous regions of North China, where his troops took hidden and protected positions in the difficult terrain. When Ch'ih Yu pursued them, his soldiers found themselves at a serious geographical disadvantage, for not only were they restricted by the terrain, but they also suffered from the cold weather, which was unfamiliar to the southerners and greatly decreased their effectiveness in combat. But the wily Ch'ih Yu was not deterred; he had his men build great fires so that smoke would envelop Hwang Ti's army, disorienting and confusing it. Only then did he order the attack. But Hwang Ti was clever enough to outwit the rebels, for he invented the magnetic compass, which enabled his forces to keep their bearings in the smoky haze and to win a decisive victory.

Hwang Ti's ideas about military strategy form the basis of the book entitled *Ch'i Men Tun Chia* (Mysterious Gate for Hiding the Army). Though actually written during the Han dynasty by Chang Liang and Chu Ko Liang, it is thought to contain an authentic account of concepts that originated in the time of Hwang Ti himself. Actually, the legend is that the ideas were revealed to Hwang Ti by a goddess. The book contains information on how to predict enemy conditions, how to plan attack and retreat maneuvers, how to conceal one's own condition from the enemy, and how to use weather phenomena in warfare. Most of this information is quite obsolete in a practical sense, and in more recent times came to have occult significance when fortune-tellers began to use its techniques to predict the destinies of individuals.

Another ancient pioneer of Taoist military strategy was Kiang Shang, who lived during the eleventh century B.C. (early antiquity, to be sure, but more than a millennium after the reign of Hwang Ti). Though he was a poor fisherman, he became the chief military adviser for King Wen and King Wu, who overthrew the tyrant Chou of the Shang Yin dynasty and founded the Chou dynasty. After their triumph, Kiang Shang was given the territory of Ch'i as a fief, and became the first duke of Ch'i. His descendants were among the most powerful nobles in China for centuries. It should be noted that in accepting this position of authority and influence, Kiang Shang acted in a way quite uncharacteristic of the early Taoists. Perhaps it is not correct to consider him a true Taoist. Yet he used Taoist principles in his strategic thought, and his early life as a simple fisherman no doubt exemplified the Taoist style of life in its solitude and independence. His ideas of strategy emphasized the methods of concealing conditions and plans from the enemy. The writing attributed to him is entitled *Lu Tao*, which means literally "Six Quivers." But "quiver" is understood to refer not merely to a container in which the archer carries (and hides) his arrows, but also to any means an army may employ to conceal its weapons or its strength from its adversaries. It is possible that Kiang Shang's strategic thought is alluded to by Lao Tzu in Chapter 36 of the *Tao Te Ching*, where it is written:[5]

Just as fish stay deep in the pond,
So the best weapons of the state are those that are not shown to the
    people.

After the time of Lao Tzu and Confucius, a more definite
concept of Taoist military strategy began to emerge. This was partly
due to the great advance in Taoist philosophy brought about by Lao
Tzu, whose own teachings on the theory of war have already been
discussed. But it was also a result of the work of Sun Wu Tzu, a
contemporary of Confucius, whose book *Sun Tzu Ping Fa* (The Art
of War by Sun Tzu) is considered by many historians and strategists
even today the greatest book on military strategy ever written. Born
in the state of Ch'i, Sun Wu Tzu became a general and military
adviser to the king of Wu, south of the Yangtze River, where he
planned many successful battles against neighboring states. But he is
most famous for his writing, the thirteen chapters of which constitute
the earliest complete treatise on military operations. In most respects,
Sun Tzu's philosophy is consistent with the ideas of Lao Tzu. But he
was far more systematic and practical in his point of view and gave
much more specific information on how to apply the basic principles
to various aspects of warfare: tactics, logistics, maneuvers, offensive
and defensive strategy, problems of terrain, and so on. Sun Tzu's art
of war guided military practice in China for centuries. Even in the
twentieth century, it had a deep influence on the thought of Mao Tse-
tung, as well as other Chinese military leaders. It has also been
translated into many languages. An English translation by Samuel B.
Griffith, a retired general of the U.S. Marine Corps, was published by
Oxford University Press in 1963. A Japanese translation has recently
become popular, particularly among Japanese businessmen, many of
whom consult it in order to apply its principles to business strategy.

During the Period of the Warring States, several people became
highly skilled Taoist military strategists as well as politicians and
statesmen. Perhaps the greatest authority on these matters during this
time was Wang Shu (Wang Li), who became known as Kuei Ku Tzu,
which means "Master of Ghost Valley." He was a real Taoist—a
shadowy, semi-legendary character who never became a general or
had a position of power, whose time and place of birth are not

precisely known, who was rumored to possess magic powers, to have lived for several hundred years, and to be immortal. Even the place where he lived, Ghost Valley, is questionable—a Chinese encyclopedia lists four distinct places in China known as Ghost Valley and locally claimed to be the location where Kuei Ku Tzu lived and taught.[6] His fame as a military strategist is entirely due to his activities as a theorist and teacher. He is thought to have put great emphasis on the idea of the alternation and opposition of Yin and Yang and to have brought the application of this idea in military and political strategy to a high level of development. Among his students during the fourth century B.C. were several who later became influential political and military leaders in the struggle for hegemony among the states that characterized this period in history. One was Su Chin, who became premier of Ch'i and leader of the so-called Vertical Alliance, a group of six states extending from south to north, united against Ch'in to the west. Another was Chang Yi, the premier of Ch'in who led the "Horizontal Alliance," which included states extending from east to west, united against Ch'i. Others were P'ang Chuan, who became a great general in the state of Wei in Central China, and Sun Pin, perhaps the grandson of Sun Wu Tzu, who became a military adviser in Ch'i.

The Period of the Warring States came to an end when the diplomatic strategy of Chang Yi broke the Vertical Alliance apart and made it possible for the powerful state of Ch'in to conquer the eastern states one by one. Finally, when the state of Ch'i fell in 221 B.C., the king of Ch'in was unchallenged and became emperor Ch'in Shih Hwang Ti, the first ruler of all China since the collapse of the Chou dynasty more than two centuries earlier. Ch'in Shih Hwang Ti was a tyrannical and oppressive ruler who believed it was necessary to control the people's activities strictly, lest rebellious movements develop in the defeated states and attempt to overthrow him. He established many laws which greatly restricted the freedoms of the people, including freedom of speech, seized and melted down their weapons, and executed many who were suspected of revolutionary tendencies. Many others were sent to the north where they were forced to work on the construction of the Great Wall, often under conditions of hardship and suffering, driven by cruel officials, or to serve in the army, guarding the northern frontier against the Mongols. After Ch'in Shih Hwang Ti died in 211 B.C., the government fell into disarray. His son, who succeeded him as emperor, was assassinated after a short time by his prime minister, and the imperial throne was inherited by Ch'in Shih Hwang Ti's grandson, who was still very young. By 210 B.C., revolutionary groups became active, and within three years the Ch'in emperor was overthrown.

The most powerful of the revolutionary leaders were Liu Pang and Hsiang Yu. Liu Pang, in origin a humble peasant, was an expert swordsman and became a leader through his ability to win the people's trust and esteem. Hsiang Yu, on the other hand, was a descendant of a great general in the state of Ch'u and had many soldiers and generals among his family and friends. He was very brave and so strong that he could lift a cauldron weighing a thousand pounds. Liu Pang and Hsiang Yu led separate armies, but they became allies for the final campaign to capture the Ch'in capital. It was their agreement that whichever of them succeeded in entering the capital city first would become the new emperor. Hsiang Yu, who led the more powerful force, decided to engage the main army of the emperor in a great battle. At the same time, Liu Pang planned to move toward the capital by a more circuitous route, hoping to avoid major confrontation with the enemy.

As it turned out, Hsiang Yu's army scored a decisive victory and routed the imperial forces. But in the meantime, Liu Pang was able to advance much more quickly toward the capital and with relatively little bloodshed, smoothing his way by means of a policy of political conciliation toward local imperial officials along his route. It was Liu Pang's army that won the race to enter the capital city. The agreement between the allies failed to hold up, however, and before long Hsiang Yu claimed power. There followed five years of fighting between them. At first, it appeared that the stronger armies of Hsiang Yu would prevail, but in the end it was Liu Pang who emerged as the victor through perseverance and the clever use of strategy. He became emperor and founder of the Han dynasty. His descendants ruled China for the next four hundred years.

A very significant factor in Liu Pang's ultimate success was the strategic advice he received from his chief military and political strategist, Chang Liang, also known as Tzu Fang. A true Taoist both in his life and in his ideas of military strategy, Chang Liang consistently showed exceptional skill and judgment in the plans he devised to make the most of Liu Pang's military and political situations. Although he did not originate the principles that guided his strategic planning, he advanced beyond the earlier Taoist military strategists in applying these principles to warfare on a much larger scale than any previously known in China. According to Ssuma Ch'ien's biography of him, Chang Liang appeared very strong and virile, but was actually as gentle as a young girl. This might seem to be a strange thing to say particularly about a great military leader, but actually it is a succinct way of describing his commitment to the philosophy of Taoism. As it is written in Chapter 28 of the *Tao Te Ching*: "When a man, though aware of his masculine strength, abides by a womanly meekness, he is content to occupy the most humble position in the world."[7]

The application of this wisdom is evident in all phases of Chang Liang's life. After Liu Pang's ultimate victory, he was in a position to become a powerful duke and rule a large, prosperous territory if he chose. Instead, he requested the title of Liu Ho (Marquis of Liu, a small and insignificant territory only a few miles from P'eng Ch'eng [Hsu Chou] where he had first met Liu Pang, and where their final victory had been won). Liu Pang was surprised at this request, and asked Chang Liang why he did not wish to rule a larger territory. Chang Liang answered, "I started my life in Hsia Pi [30 miles east of Peng Ch'eng] and I first met your majesty in Liu Ch'eng. I would be glad to settle down in a place I associate with such good memories." In truth, behind his flattery he was showing the same shrewd judgment that enabled him to achieve success in the first place. He knew that Liu Pang was well aware of his military and political skill and reasoned that if he were to accept a position of power and prestige, Liu could easily grow suspicious of his ambitions and even fear that he might attempt a coup and become emperor himself. Indeed, it was not unusual for emperors to execute their former

military leaders in order to prevent such a course of events. Chang
Liang always kept in mind that it is easier to survive in humble
circumstances than in glorious ones. Eventually, he decided to devote
himself entirely to the practice of Taoism and told Liu Pang that he
wished to give up his position and retreat to the mountains to follow
his teacher and spiritual master, Hwang Shih Kung (Ch'ih Sun Tzu),
in order to become a *hsien* (immortal). Chang Liang's life was an
outstanding example of the realization of Lao Tzu's saying, "To
accomplish great success, and then to retreat into obscurity—that is
the Tao of heaven."[8]

In military strategy, Chang Liang was a master of the tactics of
retreat, and at several crucial times in the struggle between Liu Pang
and Hsiang Yu, he applied his skill with great wisdom. When Liu
Pang first entered the Ch'in capital, he was exultant in victory and
wanted to declare himself emperor immediately and take possession
of all the riches and concubines of the imperial court. But Chang
Liang strongly advised him against such action. "Your rival Hsiang
Yu has a far superior force," he pointed out to Liu Pang, "and you
cannot compete successfully if he chooses to attack. You should leave
the treasures and beautiful ladies alone and retreat to Pa Hsang [a
small town about fifteen miles northeast of the Ch'in capital]." Liu
Pang had the good sense to follow this advice. After a short time,
Hsiang Yu's army, fresh from its victory over the Ch'in, marched on
the capital, and Hsiang Yu declared himself emperor. To Liu Pang he
gave the kingdom of Han Chung, mountainous, isolated territory
without rich farmlands or wealthy inhabitants. He himself moved to
P'eng Ch'eng, near Liu Pang's birthplace, where he set up his capital
and imperial court.

Instead of protesting, Liu Pang cheerfully accepted this outcome
and retreated to the mountains of Han with his followers. At Chang
Liang's suggestion, he went so far as to burn the wooden roads and
bridges along the sharp cliffs leading to his territory, thus causing
Hsiang Yu to believe that he had no ambition to challenge his claim
to be emperor. Actually, however, Liu Pang and Chang Liang had no
intention of giving up. In the safety of the mountains they assembled
and trained a powerful army and engaged in diplomatic maneuvers
designed to deprive Hsiang Yu of allies in the territories surrounding

his capital. After years of preparations, they suddenly emerged from the mountains, taking Hsiang Yu by complete surprise, and eventually surrounded his army. For the final battle, Chang Liang devised an ingenious psychological strategy which greatly demoralized Hsiang Yu's soldiers. Most of them were natives of a part of the state of Ch'u south of the Yangtze River. But they had been campaigning for Hsiang Yu for nearly ten years and in all that time had never been able to return to their homes. Chang Liang's idea was to select several men who knew how to play the flute and assemble them on a hill overlooking P'eng Ch'eng, where the enemy forces were preparing for the upcoming fight. There they proceeded to play a folksong of the enemy soldiers' native territory in unison. When Hsiang Yu's men heard the eerie sound, they were overwhelmed with homesickness and nostalgia, their will to fight was shattered, and they deserted in large numbers. Later on, the hill came to be known as Tzu Fang Shan, after Tzu Fang's (that is, Chang Liang's) clever strategy.

Chang Liang had not always been so gentle and so clever at military strategy. He was greatly influenced by his master, Hwang Shih Kung, also know as Ch'ih Sun Tzu (Red Pine Master), whom he eventually followed into the mountains. A famous story about how he met this master illustrates how he learned the characteristics of patience and humility as well as the principles of strategy. As a young man, Chang Liang was so outraged by the tyranny of Ch'in Shih Hwang Ti that he hired a strong man to ambush and assassinate him. The plan failed, however, and Chang Liang was forced to flee to Hsa Pei, a small town about thirty miles east of P'eng Ch'eng, where he went into hiding. One day as he crossed the Ch'i bridge there, he came upon an old man lying down. When the old man saw him, he immediately dropped his shoes under the bridge and demanded that Chang Liang go down and pick them up for him and put them on his feet. Chang Liang was annoyed by this but patiently went to retrieve the shoes. But as soon as the old man had the shoes on he took them off, threw them down again and ordered Chang Liang to pick them up again. This time Chang Liang was angry, but he decided to humor the eccentric old character and went down and got the shoes back. After he put them on the old man's feet, the old man told him,

"Young man, you are worthy to be taught," and ordered him to return to the bridge early the next morning. Chang Liang did as he was told, arriving at dawn. But the old man was there waiting already, and angrily pointed out that the young man was late. That night Chang Liang went to the bridge at midnight and waited for the old man to come again. When the old man arrived in the early morning darkness, he handed Chang Liang a book and said "Young man, if you read this, you will become the teacher of the emperor." The old man turned out to be the sage Hwang Shih Kung, and his book, the *Su Shu* (Book of Pure Counsel), contained the principles of military strategy that Chang Liang learned to apply with great success.

Liu Pang and his descendants were powerful and successful emperors who reigned over an unpredecented period of peace and prosperity that lasted more than three hundred years. By the second century A.D., however, the political situation began to deteriorate throughout the empire. There was widespread corruption, gangs of bandits roamed at will through the countryside, local dukes became more independent and fought wars against their neighbors, and there were serious attempts at revolution, such as the so-called Yellow Turban Rebellion, described in the next chapter. After A.D. 220 the empire was partitioned into three independent kingdoms: Shu (Han), Wei, and Wu.

In the kingdom of Shu, also known as the later Han dynasty, an important role was played by another great Taoist military strategist, Chu Ko Liang, military adviser and prime minister to Liu Pei, who established the kingdom in what is now Szechwan province, in the year 221. Although Liu Pei was a descendant of the Han imperial family, he had no political power and led only a small force consisting mainly of refugees when he first met Chu Ko Liang in the year 207. The latter, also known as K'ung Mien, was at that time living a simple life as an independent farmer, in typical Taoist style. But he also had a reputation as a student of military affairs and was an expert on *I Ching* divination. Over the next several years, his clever military strategy and skillful diplomacy enabled Liu Pei's army to win many victories, leading up to the establishment of his kingdom. Chu Ko

Liang then served as prime minister of Shu under both Liu Pei and his son and successor Liu Ch'an.

Chu Ko Liang was apparently an expert in the use of fire, for according to one story, he once persuaded heaven to lend him the southeast wind, and used it to help him burn an entire fleet of enemy warships in the Yangtze River, thus destroying an army of 800,000. As the story suggests, Chu Ko Liang was reputed to be able to use, in addition to standard military tactics, a variety of magical powers as strategic weapons. This may be regarded as some indication of how Taoist concepts evolved late in the Han dynasty. Magic played an important role in the Taoist cult practices that developed at this time. Chu Ko Liang practiced magic in earnest, and it is said that at the end of his life, when he realized that he was about to die, he invoked the "god of the seven stars" seeking to prolong his life "in order to be of more service to his country." Unfortunately, his attempt was unsuccessful. Nevertheless, before he died he made important contributions of several kinds. In addition to his military and diplomatic accomplishments, he invented the wheelbarrow, improved the design of lanterns, and discovered new techniques in the field of medicine. He also wrote books on divination, military strategy, and policy. After his death he became something of a folk hero, and there are many places, expecially in Szechwan Province, that bear his name because his armies fought battles or camped there.

The great accomplishments of Taoist military strategists such as Chu Ko Liang and Chiang Liang had a lasting effect on Chinese military practice, for in later centuries Taoists traditionally exerted major influence on the military thinking of the emperors, and each new dynasty could point to its own Taoist sage and military genius who masterminded its greatest triumphs in battle. Perhaps the best known of the later figures is Liu Chi (Liu Po Wen), who helped Chu Yuan Chang overthrow the tyrannical Yuan dynasty and then defeat a number of rivals, including Chen Yu Liang and Chang Ssu Ch'eng, finally enabling him to become the first Ming emperor in 1368. Actually, Liu Chi is more famous in Chinese society for his legendary prophecies and predictions than for his military accomplishments. He wrote the famous *Shao Pin Ko* (Poem of Cake), a classic divination, and several other books on prediction methods, including the methods of geomancy, a form of prediction widely used in China for the selection of burial sites. It is interesting to note that Liu Chi's expertise in the techniques of predicting the future was an important component of his skill as a military strategist. The traditional methods of divination, based on the *I Ching*, the "Five Elements," and other astrological and numerological correlations, were accepted and commonly relied on as sources of military intelligence in China since ancient times. The information obtained through the practice of divination methods could be interpreted as pertaining to enemy conditions and possible courses of action, weather conditions, and other factors relevant to strategic planning. Liu Chi was among the sages who brought these ancient methods to their highest state of development, and his fame is comparable to that of the great Shao Yung. Some of his predictions turned out to be remarkably accurate. Indeed, he is believed to have foretold the Sino-Japanese war of the 1930s nearly six centuries before it occurred.

NOTES

1. Arthur Waley, *The Way and Its Power*, New York: Grove Press, 1958, p. 211.
2. See *The Texts of Taoism (TT)*, trans. James Legge, Oxford University Press, 1891, vol. 1, p. 112.
3. *Ibid.*, p. 87.
4. *Ibid.*, p. 73.
5. See Chang Chung-yuan, *Creativity and Taoism*, New York: Harper and Row, 1970, p. 92.
6. *Ts'i Hai* (The Sea of the Phrases), Shanghai: Chung Hwa, 1947, p. 1522.
7. See *TT*, vol. 1, p. 71.
8. *Tao Te Ching*, ch. 9; see TT, vol. 1, p. 53.

CHAPTER 6
TAOISM AND REBELLION

As the preceding chapters have indicated, the political significance of Taoism in Chinese cultural history is far from simple. Rather than being a definite, coherent political philosophy, Taoism has emerged as a combination of distinct and even conflicting tendencies expressed in different ways at different times. Thus Taoists originally were uninterested and uninvolved in the affairs of government, valuing their individual freedom above all. Yet they could be and were motivated to take political action, particularly in order to rebel against oppressive rulers who took advantage of the people and limited their freedoms, or against foreign invaders. There were also periods in which Taoism was identified with the political establishment, its practices being approved and at times even organized by the emperors. But in spite of the official approval it has occasionally enjoyed, Taoism has been more often than not associated with the forces of opposition, protest, and rebellion in Chinese society.

The last chapter mentioned some individual Taoist sages who gave up their lives as hermit farmers in order to become military strategists for those seeking to overthrow tyrants. But there have also been several episodes in history in which Taoist involvement in political opposition has been on a much larger scale, taking the form of mass revolutionary movements in which violent mobs terrorized cities and overthrew rulers. Occasionally their actions were instrumental in the downfall of imperial dynasties.

Mass movements under Taoist leadership, unknown in early antiquity, developed naturally from Taoist religious sects similar to that established by Chang Tao Ling during the Han dynasty. Indeed, his "Five Bushels of Rice" religion already had aspects of a mass political movement, for he fully understood that his large band of zealous follower constituted a potentially powerful weapon and used it directly to attain his political aims. Late in the second century A.D., a much larger and more widespread revolutionary movement developed from a similar but distinct Taoist sect. It brought about one of the most powerful rebellions in Chinese history, the so-called Revolt of the Yellow Turbans.

The movement developed from a religion founded by three brothers of the Chang family. It has been conjectured that this was the same Chang family as that of Chang Tao Ling, but the truth is uncertain. In any case, their religion was very similar to his, relying as it did on miracle cures and other feats of magic to attract followers and obtaining payments from them in a similar way. The followers of the sect were known as Yellow Turbans because of their distinctive yellow head wrappings, and they regarded themselves as the forces of "Yellow Heaven." Their slogan was: "The Green [old] Heaven has died, and the Yellow Heaven is coming to power." "Green Heaven" meant the social order of the Han dynasty, which at that time was becoming increasingly weak and corrupt (the character 蒼 means "old" as well as "green").

Their leaders, the three Chang brothers, had military-sounding titles. Chang Chiao was called "General of Heaven," Chang Pao was "General of Earth," and Chang Liang was "General of Men." The sect was enormously successful and before long amassed nearly two hundred thousand followers throughout a wide area in Northern China. In A.D. 184, a full-scale rebellion against the government broke out. Many areas were overrun by mobs of Yellow Turbans who burned cities and destroyed the possessions of the privileged ruling classes. After a relatively short time, the rebellion was crushed, and the Yellow Turbans were brutally suppressed; this disorderly mob of peasants proved to be no match for the professional armies of the emperor and other authorities. Nevertheless, it had a permanent weakening effect on the social order of society and was among the factors that brought about the collapse of the Han dynasty and the subsequent partition of the empire in the Three Kingdoms period.

The revolt of the Yellow Turbans was the forerunner of many similar popular uprisings in later history. The appeal of such revolutionary movements was especially great during periods when Chinese territory was invaded and occupied by foreigners. After the fourth century, when the Five Barbarian Tribes swept across the Chinese borders from the west, north, and northeast, invasions were a continual threat; and many areas, particularly in the north, were under foreign control for long periods. At times when the Chinese government was strong and unified, such as during the Sui and T'ang dynasties, the barbarians were successfully driven out. However, as soon as the dynasty showed signs of weakness and the warlords began to fight among themselves, it was no longer possible to prevent the warlike Asian tribes from invading the northern territories once again. During the Sung dynasty, a large area was occupied by the Liao (Ch'itan Tartars). The Chin (Jurchen Tartars) advanced into central China as far as the Yangtze River, forcing the Sung emperor to flee to the south in 1126. Finally, during the thirteenth century, the Mongol tribes of Genghis Khan and his son Kublai Khan conquered the entire country, overthrowing the Sung in 1279 and establishing the Yuan dynasty.

The barbarian leaders tended to be strong and cruel rulers. In areas under their domination, the people were subject to strict government controls, which greatly limited their freedom. Under Genghis Khan and his successors, a Mongolian was assigned to every village throughout the empire in order to keep a close watch on the native Chinese and quickly suppress any suspicious political developments. The repressive policies of the barbarian governments did not prevent the growth of organized revolutionary activity, however. If anything, such activity increased as a result of repression. Secret organizations were established for the purpose of resisting and overthrowing the government. In many cases, such organizations developed from Taoist religious sects similar to the "Five Bushels of

Rice" religion, which hoped to bring about their revolutionary aims through the exercise of magical powers.

This pattern of development was not limited to the Taoist religion, though; there were similar organizations that were more Buddhist in their religious orientation. Such was the so-called Red Turbans, organized by the Buddhist monk Ying Yü under the leadership of a cloth merchant named Hsu Shou Hwei. Individually, such groups did not have the power to overthrow the government, of course. When they were discovered, their leaders were usually arrested and executed. But eventually their cumulative effect was to vex seriously the barbarian rulers and ultimately to contribute to their downfall.

This was a significant factor in the fall of the Yuan dynasty. The activity of revolutionary groups greatly increased after the year 1333, when the weak and corrupt Yuan Shun Ti became emperor. Gradually, the government became less and less able to suppress them decisively, and by 1368 the resistance was enough to enable Chu Yuan Chang to defeat and overthrow the emperor.

Among the revolutionary groups that developed during the late Yuan period was the White Lotus Association, founded by the Taoist Han Shan T'ung in the territory of Luan Ch'eng. His slogan was "There will be chaos in the world." When he and his follower Liu Fu T'ung attempted to organize military resistance against the Yuan regime, they were arrested and executed. The White Lotus sect did not disappear, however. For the next several hundred years, various branches of the religion emerged from time to time, recognizable by their white lotus symbol, their curious mixture of Taoist and Buddhist religious ideas, and their revolutionary political tendencies. During the reign of the Ming emperor T'ien Chin (1621-28) there was a White Lotus rebellion in Ch'i Chou led by Wang Shen, the Fragrant Leader, so-called because he used a special perfume made from fox scent.* After he was captured and put to death, his follower Hsu Hung Ju, the self-proclaimed King of Fu Lieh, took up the leadership

---

*The legend was that a fox spirit appeared to him and gave him a strange fragrance which would lead people to believe in his magic and become his followers. There are many fox legends in Chinese folklore, and foxes were commonly believed to

of the religion and later organized a revolution in Shantung Province. Eventually it, too, was defeated and the White Lotus religion was suppressed by the government.

The Ch'ing dynasty brought another period of foreign domination to China. Its Manchurian rulers, with their own distinctive culture and language, inspired [in the native Chinese] many of the same anti-foreign sentiments and rebellious tendencies as had the barbarian invaders of earlier centuries. Secret revolutionary groups sprang up everywhere instigating many rebellions. Several were organized by various branches of the White Lotus religion. The largest took place during the reign of the emperor Chia Ch'ing (1796–1821). Liu Tzu Hsieh and Sung Tzu Ch'ing, who were among the leaders of a White Lotus sect at that time, discovered a young boy in Honan Province who was claimed to be a direct descendant of the Ming emperors. Declaring the youth to be their leader, they attracted widespread support for their efforts to overthrow the Ch'ing emperor and restore the Ming dynasty. Although they themselves were later arrested, their followers afterward remained a threat to the government for many years, continually engaging in revolutionary actions throughout the provinces of Hupei, Szechwan, Honan, Kansu, and Shensi.

In the year 1900, another branch of the White Lotus religion became involved in a rebellion that had far-reaching consequences. Unlike the episodes described earlier in the chapter, this was not a revolt against the emperor or established government. Indeed, government soldiers eventually fought on the side of the rebel mob. The target of the rebellion was the Alliance of Eight Nations, whose members had developed settlements and business activities in China during the nineteenth century. These included the United States, Japan, Russia, England, Austria, France, Germany, and Italy.

---

be able to separate their spirits from their bodies and appear in the forms of youthful men or women. A large number of fox legends were written down by P'u Sung Ling during the seventeenth century and included in his folklore collection, *Liao Chai Chih I*. Part of this collection was translated into English by H.A. Giles under the title *Strange Stories from a Chinese Studio*. For further information, cf. E.T.C. Werner, *Myths and Legends of China*, Toronto: George G. Harrap & Co. Ltd., 1958, pp. 370–71.

Ever since the Western nations became significantly involved in Chinese affairs during the eighteenth century, xenophobia had been building up at all levels of Chinese society. The government had been defeated in a series of wars against foreign powers. They had been stripped of territories (Hong Kong and Taiwan) and of Vietnam (at that time a protectorate of China with its own king and government) and forced to make other humiliating concessions in a number of unfair treaties.

One of the consequences of these developments was that the officials of the government became implicit supporters of the Catholic religion. Catholic missionaries had arrived in China during the sixteenth century, but their activities steadily increased during the nineteenth. These priests often sought not only to win converts to the Catholic religion but also to become prosperous and influential through their efforts on behalf of those who became their followers. Thus, for example, whenever those who had become converted to Catholicism were involved in economic competition or legal disputes with other people, the priests would go to the local government officials to intercede on their behalf. As the power of the foreign governments became more and more evident, the local officials began to give in to the priests' demands and regularly granted favors to the Catholics. This was not because they themselves were in sympathy with the Catholic religion; in many cases they greatly disliked the priests, but at the same time they feared the consequences of resisting those who had the support of the foreign governments.

Such fears were not at all unreasonable, for the Westerners demonstrated in a number of incidents that they were ready to use military force to protect the privileges of their missionaries. (To mention just one example, German battleships occupied Chiao Chou Bay in Shantung Province and interfered with local trade and shipping after a German missionary was killed by peasants in 1897.) The unfairness that resulted from this situation led to widespread bitterness toward the Catholics. Among the expressions of this bitterness at the end of the nineteenth century were the activities of a branch of the White Lotus religion known as the Yi Ho Tu'an.

The Yi Ho Tu'an[1] (Rightness and Harmony Organization) was similar to the traditional Taoist religions, involving many of the same magical practices and superstitious beliefs. But in some respects it was rather unusual. For example, it was considered a fellowship of brothers, and its leader, Chang Te Cheng, was called Elder Brother-Teacher. Thus it differed from the older religions in which the leadership structure greatly elevated the social position of the master with respect to that of his disciples. This emphasis on the idea of fraternity was quite likely due to the influence of the T'ai P'ing Heavenly Kingdom, a very powerful rebellious movement of the early nineteenth century, whose ideology involved a variety of pseudo-Christian concepts. The religious title of the leader of the T'ai Ping rebellion was "Heavenly Elder Brother." In most respects, however, the Yi Ho T'uan was opposed to the methods and political aims of the T'ai P'ing Heavenly Kingdom (which will be further described later in this chapter). The principle gods, Hung Chuen Lao Tzu (Old Ancestor of Heaven) and Li Shan Lao Mu (Old Mother of Li Mountain) of Yi Ho Tu'an were rather minor figures in the Taoist pantheon. It also put great emphasis on the techniques of warfare, and its members practiced several kinds of martial arts, including a form that made use of large swords.

The organization was also known by other names as a result of its emphasis on the martial arts. It was called the Big Sword Association and in the Western world was most commonly referred to simply as the Boxers. But, in spite of this emphasis, the group could hardly be considered a disciplined, well-trained army. Its military ideas and practices were pervaded by superstition and reliance on magic. For example, the members believed that magic spells could protect them against bullets and prevent enemy guns from firing. They also thought that unmarried maidens would be able to fly into the heavens carrying red lanterns, and by waving them at ships could cause them to burn and sink.

The Yi Ho Tu'an first became active in Honan, Shantung, northern Kiangsu, and Anhwei provinces, areas where the arid climate and sandy soil make farming difficult and unrewarding. The people living there tend to be poor but strong in both mind and body. Many revolutionary movements in Chinese history got their start in these territories. In the beginning, however, the Yi Ho Tu'an was not primarily a revolutionary group, and its original aims were neither extremely anti-Catholic nor extremely anti-foreign. Rather, it sought to organize the people in order to protect their homes from bandits who roamed the countryside, since the government could not be relied on for this purpose. After a period of time, as the group grew in strength, it began to organize resistance against Catholicism and other foreign influences. Such resistance eventually became the main focus of its activities, largely as a result of its involvement in a dispute within the imperial family at the end of the nineteenth century.

At that time there developed a quarrel between the Empress Ts'i Hsi, the so-called Queen Mother of the Western Palace, and the youthful Emperor Kuang Shü. Although it had bitter personal aspects as well, the dispute had important political implications that directly concerned the impact of foreign influence on Chinese culture and life. The old empress was very conservative, and viewed the activities of foreign missionaries and businessmen as extremely destructive of valuable Chinese cultural traditions. The emperor, on the other hand, was fascinated and impressed by Western ideas, and looked with favor on new ways of thought. During a period of one hundred days in the year 1898, he issued edicts which called for sweeping reforms of society and introduction of Western practices to replace many traditional customs. The empress was so disgusted by this that she came out of retirement and asserted her power, seeking to depose Kuang Shü and put someone in his place who would be more subject to her influence. Thus a struggle for power developed in which each side had support among the government officials.

The foreign diplomatic community strongly supported Kuang Shü, of course, and this put the empress at a decided disadvantage. To increase the strength of her position, she tried to stir up the anti-foreign sentiments of the common people, hoping to mobilize widespread rebellion against foreign domination. She threw her support behind the Yi Ho Tu'an, giving official sanction to its actions and making it function as her own army. This brought about a wave of violence, in which unruly mobs under the leadership of the Yi Ho Tu'an burned Catholic churches, killed priests and their converts, and destroyed railroads, telegraph lines, Western buildings and other manifestations of "foreign evil" in many areas throughout the country.

In many cases, these mobs included gangsters, bandits, and other criminal elements that the Yi Ho Tu'an had originally been formed to protect the people against. Eventually, they reached the capital city of Peking and surrounded the area known as Tung Chiao Mien Shiang, where the embassies and homes of the foreign diplomats were located. When a number of terrified foreigners and Catholics took refuge in the Catholic cathedral, a mob threatened to storm it, and French troops stationed nearby had to rush to their rescue.

The situation drew to a climax on June 20, 1900, when the German minister Freiherr von Ketteler, on his way to meet with the Chinese Minister of Foreign Affairs, was captured and killed by the rebel crowd. This event provoked the foreign governments to respond with military force. Allied warships were sent to the seaport city of T'ientsin, and troops landed and marched toward the Chinese capital. The Chinese government deployed two divisions of regular army troops to resist the invasion, but neither they nor the disorganized Yi Ho Tu'an peasants could prevent the foreign allies from reaching Peking. The government fled to Sian in Shensi province and was forced to make indemnity payments by the terms of the treaty signed the following year, the so-called Year of the Shein Shou Treaty. This affair was known in the West as the Boxer Rebellion.

The geographical area where the Yi Ho Tu'an originated—comprising parts of Honan, Shantung, Kiangsu, and Anhwei provinces—was for centuries the most fertile territory in all of China for the growth of Taoist religious and political organizations. Rebellions were spawned there at many different times in history. This was no mere coincidence, for the conditions favorable for the success of Taoist magicians and religious leaders, such as willingness to believe in magic and folk superstitions, were habits deeply rooted in the historical traditions of the people living in the area. In ancient times, the region was a center of the Shang Yin civilization, and during the Spring and Autumn Period it was the territory of the state of Sung, whose capital was at Shang Chiu (now in Eastern Honan). The duke of Sung was a descendant of the Shang Yin dynasty, which had been overthrown during the twelfth century B.C. Still, its culture had survived among the people in the area, especially in the form of folk superstitions and magic practices. The region was also central in

Taoist history. Chang Tao Ling, the creator of the Taoist religion, was born there; he was an eighth-generation descendant of the great Taoist military strategist Chang Liang. In the preceding chapter we mentioned that Chang met the old Taoist Hwang Shih Kung there and later was given the fief Liu in the area. Even Lao Tzu is believed to have dwelt in this region, in a place called P'ei Hsien, where Confucius is said to have visited him; another Taoist, Yang Chu, found him in the suburb of P'ei.[2]

The peculiar cultural heritage of this region of China could be felt in the attitudes and life styles among the people there, even in relatively recent times. In fact, it was an important factor in my own personal experience, for I grew up near Hsuchou, in the midst of this region, during the early decades of this century. As a youth, I witnessed the development of a Taoist religious rebellion that had most of the typical features of the great rebellions of earlier times in history. The organization involved was popularly known as the Red Spear Association, also called the Pa Kua Chiao (Eight Trigrams Religion). Its own members referred to it as the Li religion, after the trigram Li ($\equiv$), which was its special symbol. In the traditional symbolism of the *I Ching*, this trigram represents fire, and its characteristic color is red. The members could be identified by the red-tasseled spears they carried.

The Li trigram also figured in propaganda put out by the organization, such as the slogan:

> The religion of Li is in the Southern direction.
> Here is a ladder you can climb to Heaven.
> The gods of this religion hold the steering-pole of Heaven.

Like the slogan of the Yellow Turbans, this saying proclaims the belief of its members that the religion represents the powers of Heaven, which would rule the earth through its actions. The slogan refers to King Wen's arrangement of the trigrams, in which the trigram Li appears in the southern position. In its use of the symbolism of the traditional culture for propaganda purposes, the Red Spear Association followed the typical pattern of Taoist rebellions since ancient times.

The Red Spear Association also practiced magic, including miracle cure techniques, with the aim of attracting followers, just as did Taoist religious and political leaders of earlier centuries. Unlike some of the earlier sects, however, the Red Spear Association did not try to stir up a major rebellion or advocate the overthrow of the government. Its political purposes were mainly to organize the people to protect their homes against bandits and foreigners and to preserve the traditional customs against modern tendencies. It was founded during the eighteenth century by Kao Yü Wen, who was executed as a rebel during the reign of the Emperor Ch'ien Lung. His magic was secretly preserved by his descendants for several generations, however. It finally emerged when the Red Spear Association revived and became successful in the early years of the Chinese republic. The practices of the Red Spear Association included not only magic but also martial arts and meditation. To its followers, it offered protection, increased physical and spiritual strength, and freedom from sickness through magic techniques.

By the 1920s, the sect had thousands of followers and began to spread to other regions of China. The center of its influence was a small fortified village in the suburbs of the ancient city of Shang Chiu, about sixty miles from my home, where the leader of the religion lived with members of his clan. In 1927 it suffered a disaster when a night attack by the forces of General Feng Yu Shan totally obliterated the village with heavy artillery shelling. The Red Spear Association was not destroyed, however, for it had many disciples in other territories who preserved its organization and practices. After the Communist revolution in China, some of them, including Master Liu P'ei Chung, fled to Taiwan. There, the religion became very successful, attracting thousands of followers, building large temples, and raising a great deal of money. But the name "Red Spear Association" and the insignia from which it was derived were no longer used.

An interesting feature of the Red Spear Association was its use of magic for self-defense in fighting. Like the members of the Yi Ho Tu'an, the members of the Red Spear Association believed they could protect themselves against the methods of modern warfare by magic techniques that would, among other things, render rifle bullets harmless against them. Those who practiced these techniques swore an oath of secrecy, but they apparently involved a process by which the skin was gradually toughened. In early stages of the process, the body was beaten with sticks. Later, the skin was chopped with knives, and magic spells were used to prevent the wounds from bleeding. Whether this process actually succeeded in making the skin tough enough to prevent wounds from bullets I cannot say on the basis of my own observation, although I did witness remarkable feats in which members moved heavy objects by pressing their bare chests against the sharp points of spears. There was one old master, however, whose nickname was "Iron Jacket" and whose immunity against bullet wounds had been witnessed by many people. Of course there are those who might be skeptical about this kind of magic, especially in view of the devastating artillery attack against Shang Chiu. But such a viewpoint is far too narrow if it is allowed to obscure the genuine value of many of the methods of the Red Spear Association. There is no doubt that the regular practice of meditation, martial arts, and healing methods it fostered among its members led to real physical and spiritual development.

To conclude this chapter, it should perhaps be emphasized that Taoism was far from the only ideology from which rebellions sprang during Chinese history. In fact, the characteristics we have mentioned in describing the Taoist rebellions—use of magic and folk superstitions and opposition to foreign ideas—were features that distinguished Taoist political opposition from that based on other ideologies. This can be appreciated by considering the example of the T'ai P'ing Heavenly Kingdom, a nineteenth-century religion that developed into a popular rebellion of great magnitude.

Founded by Hung Hsiu Ch'uan in Kwangsi Province, it did not develop from a genuine branch of Christianity. Its founder adopted many aspects of Christian mythology, which he had learned from Western missionaries and their writings. The religion spread quickly through many parts of China and emerged as a major rebellion, whose army of millions was a real threat to the Man-Chiang imperial government. By 1851 it controlled enough territory that Hung Hsiu Ch'uan was able to organize his own government with its capital in Nanking. Although the T'ai P'ing army never succeeded in overthrowing the emperor, the rebellion was very difficult to control, requiring many years to suppress. In some ways, the T'ai P'ing rebellion may seem to fit the pattern of Taoist rebellions described above. Yet in political terms, the contrast between them cannot be overemphasized. Unlike the Taoists, the T'ai P'ing leaders had no use for magic and folk superstitions. Indeed, they opposed all the traditional practices and beliefs of Chinese culture, including the philosophy of Confucius. At the same time they welcomed foreign influence and adopted many Western ideas. It is clear that they represented just the sort of political tendencies most strongly opposed by the Taoists.

NOTES

1. Information on the Yi Ho Tu'an is largely derived from Tai Hsuan Chieh's "Study and Research on the Yi Ho Tu'an" (in Chinese), Taiwan: Commercial Press, 1963.
2. See *The Writings of Chuang Tzu*, chs. 14 and 27; *The Texts of Taoism*, trans. James Legge, Oxford University Press, 1891, vol. 1, p. 354 and vol. 2, p. 147.

CHAPTER 7
TAOIST MAGIC

The practice of magic has played an important part in Taoist religion ever since Chang Tao Ling founded the first Taoist sect, during the Han dynasty. Indeed, magic no doubt had firm roots in Taoist tradition long before that time. As previous chapters have indicated, Taoist priests and religious organizers relied on spells and magic techniques to attract financial backers and advance their own political ambitions. These techniques included secret words and sayings, talismans and charmed objects, breath-control methods, and the like. By such means—similar to the magic and witchcraft of other cultures—they would attain public notoriety by producing spectacular events, invoking the help of the gods, and banishing evil spirits and ghosts.

The success of those who have practiced such magical arts traditionally has depended on their ability to divert and manipulate the imagination of the observer. Novelty has long been an attention getter, so the history of Taoist magic abounds with variations on basic tricks and methods, all evolving with independent originality from countless sites throughout China. Nonetheless, trickery and novelty have not been ends in themselves.

To understand correctly the role of magic in Taoism, it is important to keep in mind that it was never considered as merely a technique to impress crowds with clever effects or to lure them into accepting political propaganda. Rather, magic has always been an integral dimension of Taoist experience, affecting many Taoist practices. Thus, for example, the Taoist physicians traveling about the Chinese countryside used many methods with genuine curative value in their treatment of diseases, but also used magic spells, which had the advantage of costing nothing to practice. Taoists who aspired to achieve immortality practiced meditation, health exercises, and other longevity techniques, but also relied on magic spells. Taoist military strategists used the principles of warfare described in the classic writings to defeat the enemy, but magic tricks were also among their arsenal of weapons. The traditional Taoists did not draw a sharp distinction between practices that involve magic and those that do not. Indeed, within the ancient tradition of Taoism, there developed a view of the world that was essentially magical.

Detailed information about the magical techniques practiced by Taoists before the Han dynasty is difficult to find, but many old sources indicate that the practice of magic goes back as far as Hwang Ti, the Yellow Emperor, and perhaps even earlier. According to the *Ch'i Men Tun Chia*,[1] a goddess appeared to Hwang Ti during his war against Ch'ih Yu and gave him a book containing many secrets of strategy by means of which he was able to train wild beasts such as bears and tigers to fight together as soldiers. The *Nei Ching*, Hwang Ti's medical treatise,[2] suggests that some forms of magic were known even before his time, for the chapter entitled "Su Wen" contains the remark that "in ancient times, they cured diseases, transformed sperm into *chi* (vital energy) and divined the causes of disease by praying to the gods." The last phrase—that is, *Chu Yu K'o*, "Praying [to the Gods] to divine the cause [of Disease]—later became the title of an important book on the use of magic to cure disease, which will be further discussed below.

Among other accounts of magic in early antiquity are the legends about the great flood that inundated the empire during the time of Yao (c. 2350 B.C.) and how Yü, the minister of Shun, finally succeeded in controlling the waters and removing the obstructions that prevented them from escaping to the sea in 2283 B.C. The flood itself and the efforts of Yü, who later succeeded Shun as emperor and came to be known as "Yü the Great," are described in the *Shu Ching*.[3] Meng Tzu also mentions these events, and his account[4] includes a description of how the waters that flooded the land contained large snakes and dragons, which then occupied the territory and forced all the people away, and how Yü the Great subdued these monsters, forcing them into grassy marshes where they could do no harm to the people. Neither of these classics gives a detailed account of just how Yü was able to accomplish this, but many old legends suggest that his methods were at least partly magical.

The *San Hai Ching* (Book of the Mountains and Seas), a Chin dynasty work by the author Kuo P'u, contains descriptions and pictures of large, strange-shaped monsters, which would obviously require extraordinary means to be conquered.

Though these descriptions are probably mostly legend, discoveries of fossilized bones of large reptiles in China and elsewhere suggest the legend may be based on the actual history of a much earlier period. In any case, the stories of Yü the Great indicate that he invoked the help of the gods by the use of magic and by their help was able to conquer the sea monsters and then control them, employing their great strength to penetrate the obstructions in the mountains so that the waters could flow down to the sea.

It is known from the *Shu Ching* that Yü put great emphasis on the five elements (earth, water, fire, wood, and metal), the fundamental processes of which the universe in constituted. The five elements, when the Yin (female) and Yang (male) aspects of each are distinguished, comprise the Ten Heavenly Stems, which combine with the Twelve Earthly Branches (that is, the twelve animals of the zodiac) to represent the total of 60 stages of the sexagenary calendar cycle. In later Taoist religion, these sixty combinations of stems and branches were personified as gods and goddesses. Six gods (or goddesses) were thus associated with each of the ten Heavenly Stems. The six gods of Chia (male wood) and the six goddesses of Ting (female fire) were believed to possess magic powers that enabled them to subdue dragons, move mountains, and perform other miraculous feats. According to popular belief, it was Yü's ability to summon the powers of these twelve that enabled him to overcome the dangers and solve the problems of the great flood.

The deeds of Yü the Great are common knowledge throughout China today, and especially in a number of places whose names commemorate them. For example, the place where the Yellow River flows through the mountains between Shensi and Shansi provinces is called Yü Men (Yü's Gate) because Yü is believed to have made the cut in the mountains there for the water to escape. And near Changsha, in Hunan Province, I have seen a large stone tablet halfway up the side of Yoh Lu Mountain with some strange characters carved on it. No one is sure how the tablet got there, but it is called the Tablet of Emperor Yü, and the traditional belief is that there was once a deep cave in the mountainside and Yü the Great, after subduing a giant serpent, thrust it into the cave and covered the entrance with the stone so that it would never be able to escape.

After the reign of Yü the Great, which (according to the historical tradition) ended in 1783 B.C., China was ruled for about six hundred years by the Shang Yin dynasty. There is considerable archaeological evidence about the culture of this period, for many tombs of the Shang Yin emperors have been discovered near Anyang and excavated. Among the artifacts found in these tombs were animal bones and other objects used in divination; and by deciphering inscriptions carved on them it has been discovered that the emperors put great stock in these predictions, which concerned such events as wars, hunting expeditions, festivals, and agricultural conditions. It is also reasonable to suppose that they were interested in magic, but no historical records give any detailed account of what the magical practices and techniques during this period might have been.

There are a great many stories about the fall of the Shang Yin dynasty and the wars in which King Wu defeated the tyrant Hsin Chou and founded the Chou dynasty. Several of these tell of magic powers and miraculous devices used as weapons during this fighting. A major source of this information is the *Feng Chen Chuan*, also known by the title *Feng Shen Yen I*. It dates from the Ming dynasty, and its author is unknown. Comprising more than 100 chapters, this book is perhaps most accurately thought of as a dictionary of the gods and goddesses of Taoism and Buddhism. It contains a great deal of information, mostly legendary, about the fall of the Shang Yin and other events in early history because many of the prominent soldiers who fought and died in the great battles were later promoted to the status of gods and their exploits exaggerated in a way that was appropriate to their status as deities.

According to these accounts, the generals on both sides in this great war were students of Buddhist and Taoist immortals who taught them how to use magic techniques. For example, Kiang Shang (also known as Kiang Tzu-Ya), the principal military adviser of King Wu was a disciple of the great Taoist immortal Yuan-Shi T'ien Tsun. Among the magic techniques and devices described in the book are a mirror that could be used to concentrate light rays on distant objects, causing them to catch fire; a fan that could be used to blow fire quickly over great distances; umbrellas that could float down from the sky, spreading deadly diseases over a wide area; a wind-fire wheel that could be ridden, capable of traveling at great speed; and a technique of traveling through the air by riding on clouds.

It may be reasonably assumed that the practice of magic and witchcraft continued during the later Chou dynasty and the Period of the Warring States, at the same time as the philosophical classics of Taoism were being written. Though the great Taoist philosophers did not put much emphasis on magic, their occasional allusions to extraordinary powers and strange feats suggest that they were aware of it. In the *Chuang Tzu*, for example, there is a statement to the effect that the "true men" of ancient times, who really knew the Tao, could pass through water without getting wet and could go into fire without being burnt.[5] Another famous example, mentioned in the *Chuang Tzu* and many other sources, concerns the Taoist immortal Lieh Tzu, who had the ability to travel through the air by riding the wind.[6] These are merely literary allusions, however, and almost nothing is known about the precise state of the arts of magic during this time.

It is probably true that the famous burning of the books by Ch'in Shih Hwan Ti in 210 B.C. had particularly destructive results for writings about magic. The superstitiousness of this emperor and his enthusiasm for magic have often been mentioned by historians. It is also well-known that he was greatly worried about the possibility that his enemies might assassinate him, perhaps even by the use of black magic. At any rate, none of the treatises on magic and techniques and practices that may have existed in the third century B.C. survive today.

For later periods in history, during and after the Han dynasty, there is enough available information to provide a somewhat clearer view of magic beliefs and practices than that which can be constructed from the vague legends of earlier times. Even in talking about quite recent times, it is necessary to rely on legends, of course, for the practice of magic is essentially mysterious, and successful magicians never reveal their actual methods. Nevertheless, certain historical generalizations can be reliably formulated. One is that the practice of magic in China after the second century B.C. was considerably influenced by techniques and ideas that originated in Central Asia. Travelers such as Chang Ch'ien, who was sent to Central Asia as an envoy of Emperor Han Wu Ti (140–97 B.C.), brought back accounts of rope tricks, escape artists, fire breathing, exchanging the heads of horses and oxen, and other magic feats they observed. The *So Shen Ji* (Record of the Exploits of the Gods), published in A.D. 350, states that many magic sayings and techniques originated in India.

By the late Han period, these methods were adopted and given a distinct Chinese character. This can be surmised from accounts of the magic practiced by the Taoist religious leader Chang Tao Ling (2d century A.D.), about whom one can obtain a reasonably substantial account of his career as a magician and the sources of his magic practices. Chang Tao Ling was born in the Pei area near Hsuchou in what is now Kiangsu Province. Early in his life he became interested in meditation and alchemy, and after a time he journeyed to Szechwan, where materials such as mercury and cinnabar needed for alchemical study were easier to obtain than in other places. While in Szechwan, he lived in a cave on the Ho Ming Shan (Whooping Crane Mountain). There he is said to have met the immortal Lao Tzu. Lao Tzu taught him many techniques and gave him writings related to the practice of magic as well as two swords which had magic powers.

The teachings he obtained from Lao Tzu essentially concerned the ghosts and evil spirits who bring about disease, death, and other kinds of misfortune for humans, and how to conquer and control them in order to save lives and prevent suffering. According to these teachings, the world of ghosts and spirits is governed by relationships similar to those which prevail in human society (that is, the empire). Furthermore, the efforts of the evil spirits to harm people are to be understood and responded to in military terms. That is, there are six ghost kings, and each of them rules over a vast army of ghost soldiers through a structure of officials and generals. In order to prevent harm it is necessary to conquer these ghost armies and defeat the plans of the evil ghost kings. According to Chang Tao Ling, the teachings he received from Lao Tzu enabled him to use magic sayings and writing to control the spirits so that they served as heavenly soldiers, fighting against the ghost armies and preventing them from achieving their evil purposes.

There are many indications that Chang Tao Ling was able to put these ideas into effect with great success. Not only was he able to work many miracle cures, which attracted to him a large following, but there are many stories of other miraculous events he brought about by the use of magic. For instance, he once drove away a white tiger-god whose thirst for human blood led it to terrorize a region near Ho Ming Mountain. On another occasion, he subdued a large serpent, whose breath was like a poisonous mist that had killed many people.

The methods of curing diseases by magic were actually used by Chang Tao Ling and other Han dynasty Taoists. These may be reconstructed on the basis of information to be found in the book *Chu Yu K'o* (Praying [to the Gods] to divine the cause [of Disease]). The origin and authorship of this book are shrouded in mystery. Legend has it that it was discovered during the twelfth century A.D. by the Sung dynasty official Ch'uo Ch'i while he was dredging the Yellow River. Ch'uo Ch'i was convinced that the book was very ancient and attributed its authorship to Hwang Ti. While this was almost certainly a great exaggeration, there is reason to suppose that the magic described in the book was already known and practiced many centuries earlier than the Sung dynasty. The *Chu Yu K'o* contains many magic sayings, symbols, and strange written characters that can be applied to cure a great variety of maladies. These methods are known to have been used in recent times and perhaps survive even today in certain remote areas of China. They were especially popular in the Chen Chou (Yuan Ling) region of Hunan Province, where high-quality cinnabar (a substance needed for magic writing and in other magic procedures) was readily available, and in the mountainous area between Kwei Chou and Szechwan provinces, where the Miao tribesmen and other ethnic minorities preserved many folk superstitions. In these territories, magic practices were known to almost everyone and taken seriously even by educated persons.

Some years ago, an article about the magic practices in this region appeared in the biographical magazine *Chuan Chi Wen Hsueh*.[7] The author, a native of Tsun Yi in northern Kwei Chou province, China, was Liu Chien Ch'un, formerly president of the legislative Yuan of the Chinese republic on Taiwan. The article was in part a report of his own experience, for his father had been cured of a serious wound by the magician Li Ch'un Shien. In addition, the article reported that witch doctors in his native area had been known to remove warts and tumors from people and transfer them to plants and animals by means of magic sayings. They were said even to perform operations, opening the abdominal cavity with their fingernails, taking out the inner organs and washing the sickness away. After returning them to the body, they allegedly closed the wounds so that they healed immediately, leaving no scars and without causing any pain. Another eyewitness account reported in this article concerns a magician who was able to remove a bullet from a person's arm by tapping a small hammer on a wooden door and calling for the bullet to come out.

Chang Tao Ling is by no means the only late Han dynasty magician whose miracles are still remembered today. Indeed, Chang Tao Ling's importance as a historical figure is mainly a result of his skill as a religious and political organizer. Others were even more renowned for their magic skills and marvelous feats. Such was Tso Tz'u (A.D. 155–220), considered one of the greatest miracle-workers in China.[8]

There are many popular stories about the exploits of Tso Tz'u.

Several have to do with his demonstrations of magic at the instigation of the powerful premier Ts'ao Ts'ao. It is said that when he first appeared before Ts'ao Ts'ao, claiming to be a magician, the premier tested him by locking him in a room for an entire year, during which he did not give him any food or water. At the end of the year, the room was opened and Tso Tz'u emerged, alive and perfectly fit. This greatly impressed the premier Ts'ao Ts'ao, and the magician was allowed to go free. On a later occasion, the premier invited a hundred people to a feast. At the last moment, he was disappointed to discover that his servants had been unable to obtain any Lu fish from the Sung Chiang River, a delicacy he planned to serve his guests for the main course. When Tso Tz'u found out about this, he got a washtub, filled it with water and began to catch Lu fish in it with a hook and line. Before long, more than enough fish had been obtained to feed all the guests. Then, in order to obtain some ginger so that the fish could be properly spiced, Tso Tz'u threw a goblet into the air, where it magically turned into a white crane, which flew off and later returned with some high-quality ginger from Szechwan. Finally, Tso Tz'u brought out a small bottle and began to pour wine from it for the guests to drink. Before the bottle was empty, everyone at the feast had gotten drunk.

Demonstrations of magic powers such as this made the premier Ts'ao Ts'ao somewhat ambivalent toward Tso Tz'u. On the one hand, he greatly admired the magician's technique; but on the other hand, he became afraid that Tso Tz'u might use his powers to kill or harm him. At length, he decided to kill the magician in order to get rid of these worries. But just as Tso Tz'u was about to be captured by the premier's men, he vanished by walking through a wall. After that, he was occasionally seen and pursued by the authorities but always escaped by means of magic. One time he was observed in a crowded marketplace, but when the soldiers arrived, all the people in the market appeared to have been transformed so that they were indistinguishable from Tso Tz'u. Since it was impossible to tell which of them was the "real" Tso Tz'u, no one could be arrested. At another time, Tso Tz'u was seen in the mountains and the premier's men were summoned. But the magician transformed himself so that he appeared to be a sheep, mixed in with the flocks grazing on the mountainside, and so escaped once again.

Tso Tz'u eventually passed his knowledge of magic on to many students. Perhaps the most famous of them was Ko Hsuan, also known as Ko Hsien Wong (Old Immortal), a native of the town of Tan Yang in the territory of Wu during the Three Kingdoms periods. Ko Hsuan was a key figure in the development of Taoist religion, for he was believed to have experienced several visions, in which writings were revealed to him by the Ruler of Heaven (T'ai Shang) and other gods. These divinely inspired works and other writings by him became important devotional classics of Taoism (see page 24). But in addition, Ko Hsuan was well-known for his skill as a magician, which he learned mainly from Tso Tz'u.

Like his teacher, he apparently enjoyed performing magic tricks for the entertainment of dinner guests. According to one story, he terrified a group of people by turning a bowl of cooked rice into a swarm of angry bees. As the guests scrambled to get away from the threatening swarm, Ko Hsuan opened his mouth wide, and all the bees flew inside and changed back into rice again. On another occasion, he is said to have caused wine goblets to move from the table to his guests' mouths spontaneously, without being lifted or touched in any way.

But other stories suggest that Ko Hsuan used magic not only for entertainment but to help people out and rescue them from difficulties. Once, as he was riding in a chariot, he came upon a crowd of people outside a temple who warned him not to go too close, for the temple had been taken over by an evil demon. "You should get out of your chariot a hundred feet away and bow down to the demon if you don't want to come to any harm," they said. When he heard this, Ko Hsuan took a piece of paper and wrote some magic characters on it. Then he rode his chariot right up to the temple and flung the piece of paper inside. Suddenly, an explosion was heard, and flames and smoke came out of the temple. After that, the evil demon was never heard from again. According to another story, Ko Hsuan once visited the home of a family in which one of the members was seriously ill. A witch doctor had sensed the presence of an evil demon, and told the people that they should make sacrificial offerings to appease it if they hoped for a cure. But Ko Hsuan had a better idea. By means of a magic saying, he summoned a ghost and ordered it to whip the demon as punishment for the harm it was causing. After a time, the demon emerged from its hiding place, black and blue from the whipping, knelt and bowed down in front of Ko Hsuan to beg forgiveness for its evil deeds.

These stories, as well as others already mentioned, illustrate the extent to which the traditional Chinese attitude toward magic has emphasized its potential use to benefit people and save them from harm. Throughout history, the average person in China has been at the mercy of natural processes and aware at all times of his vulnerability to such disasters as floods, famines, and pestilence. It is easy to appreciate that he has always been attracted by the idea that certain men have magic powers which enable them to control nature, making it conform to their wishes. What could be more natural for those who were masters of these mysterious arts (provided that they were men of virtue) than to use their skills for the benefit of those who were not so fortunate? Such an idea underlies many examples of magic beliefs in Chinese culture—from the legends of Yü the Great, who used magic to control the great flood, to the mass appeal enjoyed by Chang Tao Ling and other practitioners of miracle cure techniques. But there is probably no better example of this than the story of Hsu Hsun, a man of the highest character, a public official under the Chin dynasty (A.D. 265–420) who eventually became an immortal with an important place in the Taoist pantheon.

Hsu Hsun was a native of Nan Ch'ang in Kiangsi Province, where beginning at an early age he studied the classics. It is said he was deeply affected by an experience he had as a youth, when he shot a young fawn and then witnessed the mother deer grieving over its death. Horrified by the suffering he had brought about, he no longer went hunting and put most of his energy into learning. He was especially interested in Taoism, and became a student of the Taoist master Wu Meng, from whom he learned the techniques of meditation, alchemy, and magic. (According to some accounts, he may have studied with the magician Tso Tz'u.) But unlike many who became preoccupied with Taoist interests and dropped out of official society, he held a position of responsibility as prefect of Ching Yang in Szechwan for many years, going into retirement only when the government began to disintegrate in the declining years of the Chin dynasty.

As a government official, he earned fame and admiration because of his great concern for the people and extraordinary means he employed to alleviate their sufferings in the face of disaster. The year after he was appointed to the prefecture, there was a major crop failure in the region and all the farmers were wiped out. Many faced starvation, and almost none had any hope of being able to pay the annual land taxes they owed the government. In response to this situation, Hsu Hsun decreed that all who were unable to pay their taxes would be required to serve as laborers on a public works project in the district. Then he used a magic spell to transform a substantial quantity of iron into gold and hid it in the ground where these people would be working. When the workers discovered the gold, they were overjoyed at their good fortune and were able to buy food and pay their taxes. None of them suspected that the gold had been put there as a result of Hsu Hsun's magic.

At about the same time there was an epidemic of a deadly disease in the area, and many people died. When it became clear that it was a great danger to the public health, Hsu Hsun ordered a large quantity of water to be collected and brought to him. Then he cast a magic spell on the water and indicated that it was for the sick to drink. Those who drank it found that they were miraculously cured of the disease. The magic water was widely distributed, not only in the territory of Ching Yang but in neighboring areas as well, and many lives were saved.

The historical accounts of the prefecture of Hsu Hsun emphasize the many successful public projects accomplished under his leadership. He was always dredging the rivers and building dikes for flood control and bridges to aid in transportation. These projects made heavy use of manpower, of course, but there are many stories which tell of his use of magic to overcome evil dragons, which are always associated with storms and floods in Chinese folklore.

According to one such story, he was able to slay dragons because a goddess appeared to him and gave him a magic sword to use as a weapon. Other stories about Hsu Hsun are reminiscent of the legends of Yu the Great. These stories became so popular that even today, many places are named after magic feats he is believed to have accomplished there.

Among Hsu Hsun's accomplishments was the founding of a religious sect, the Ching Ming Chung Chiao, which later evolved into the southern branch of Taoist religion. He is also famous for having practiced meditation with his entire family. This was quite unusual, since most who practiced meditation were either solitary hermits or living in monastic communities. It is said that he lived to be 136, after which he and his entire family became immortal. Eventually, he was worshipped as a god of the Taoist religion and given the title Chen Chun (True King of the Taoists). In the Heavenly Palace, he was considered an important officer of the Jade Emperor, often visualized as guarding the gates of heaven.

The reign of the Chin dynasty, during which Hsu Hsun lived, was an uneasy period in many respects. It was a time when five barbarian invasions conquered many parts of China and governmental authority was often unstable. Comparing the cycle of historical change in Chinese culture to the annual cycle of the seasons, it can be said that whereas the Han dynasty was like the spring and summer, the Three Kingdoms Period was like the autumn and the later Chin dynasty the dead of winter. Yet in spite of the general cultural decline during the Chin period, some important contributions were made, of which Hsu Hsun's was only one example.

During this period there was increasing contact with the culture of India. Many highly developed and sophisticated magic practices that originated in India found their way into China, along with the literature, religious ideas, and other aspects of Indian civilization. This had the effect of further stimulating the Chinese enthusiasm for magic, which was already very popular as a result of the rapid development of indigenous Chinese methods and practices. Some of the magic lore of the period can be found in such writings as the *Sou Shien Chi* (Reports on Spiritual Manifestations) by Kan Pao, which appeared in A.D. 348 and the *Shen Hsien Chuan* (Lives of the Divine Hsien), an early fourth-century work attributed to Ko Hung.

Among the magicians who became famous during this time in addition to Hsu Hsun, most worthy of mention is Kuo P'u (A.D. 276–324), who, like Hsu Hsun, studied with the Taoist immortal Wu Meng. Accounts of his magic powers include the story that when he threw beans into the air, they would change into soldiers or ghosts who would carry out his commands. In addition to performing such tricks, Kuo P'u was an expert on divination methods and geomancy. He wrote many books on these techniques, notably the *I Tung Lin* (Grottoes and Forests of the Book of Changes). In later times his writings were often consulted by Taoist priests who practiced these techniques.

The reunification of the entire territory of China under the Sui dynasty in the year 581 marked the beginning of a cultural renaissance. The high point of this development came during the reign of the T'ang dynasty (618–960), an extended time of peace and prosperity comparable to the Han dynasty period as a golden era of Chinese civilization. Possessing sufficient military strength, the people did not have to fear foreign invasions. The Chinese of this period, therefore, acted as a powerful cultural influence on other Asian peoples—particularly the Japanese, who came to China by the thousands to travel and study.

The official respect enjoyed by Taoism (and Buddhism) during the T'ang dynasty has already been noted in a previous chapter. As a result of it, such Taoist practices as meditation, alchemy, and magic became very popular, and a great many people achieved highly advanced levels of development in these arts. At the highest levels were those who actually achieved immortality as *hsien*.[9] Although quite a number of Taoists are believed to have reached this goal during the T'ang period, most are unknown to later historians. A few became very famous, however, and none more so than the so-called Pa Hsien (Eight Immortals). Among the most popular subjects of representation in Chinese art, they were adored in a special way both as a group and individually. There is such a wealth of legend and romance about the Eight Immortals that without writing a rather lengthy book devoted to them alone, it is barely possible to indicate their role in Chinese culture. Each of the Eight Immortals was believed to possess unique magic powers all his own. Together they represented a remarkable cross-section of T'ang society, including both men and women, old and young, rich and poor. More about the Eight Immortals is to be found in later chapters. Here we must limit our account to mere sketches of a few stories about two of them—Lu Tung Pin and Chang Kuo—simply to suggest their personalities and illustrate the magic powers associated with them and involved in their cult.

The benevolent, somewhat grandfatherly Lu Tung Pin was among the best loved of Chinese folk heroes. His original name was Lu Yen, and he is also known by the Taoist title Ch'un Yang Tzu, which means The Pure Yang Master—that is, without any Yin. To the peasants he was every bit as famous and important as Confucius or Chang Tao Ling. Born during the eighth century into a family of officials, he spent most of his life practicing Taoist methods. He is credited with consolidating the various rather disorganized aspects of Taoist religion at that time into a coherent unified whole. His efforts provided a concept of orthodoxy and correctness that influenced Chinese society and other Asian countries. As part of his system, he adopted many Buddhist ideas, particularly those of Ch'an (Zen) Buddhism. But while these accomplishments made him famous, he is far better known for his activities after attaining immortality. He would appear from time to time throughout the centuries, often helping those who were in trouble by exercising his magic powers, but without revealing his identity to them. Sometimes he would show up in wine shops, drink wine with people, and entertain them by composing wonderful poems. He was believed able to fly, for there were verified instances in which he was seen on one side of Tung T'ing Lake in the morning, and then on the opposite side, some 300 miles away, in the evening of the same day.

An important aspect of the cult of Lu Tung Pin involves a technique of divination using sand and willow sticks. Known as Chi divination, it is traditionally done with an apparatus consisting of a bed of sand over which an object is suspended. A willow stick capable of writing in the sand is attached to the suspended object, which is then swung or moved about. Its use is usually connected with veneration of Lu Tung Pin, although other gods may also be involved. The divination apparatus is called a Chi T'an and is used in the following way.

After magic incantations are recited summoning Lu Tung Pin and other gods to appear and work their magic, two blindfolded persons move the suspended object, automatically creating a pattern of markings in the sand below. The markings can be interpreted either as a picture or as Chinese characters forming a saying or poem. It is possible, by repeated application of the method, to obtain lengthy statements or even whole books in this way. In practice, the interpretation is usually used for fortune telling and can be considered either an answer to a specific question or a comment about an existing situation or set of circumstances. According to a legend, Lu Tung Pin appeared at a Chi T'an sometime during the seventeenth century and wrote a lengthy discourse. A now-forgotten Taoist copied down the characters and published the resulting manuscript under the title *T'ai I Chin Hua Tsung Chih* (The Secret of the Golden Flower). It became one of the best-known treatises on Taoist meditation and in recent times has been translated into Western languages and read throughout the world.[10]

There are many versions of the story of how Lu Tung Pin achieved immortality, but it is generally agreed he learned the necessary secrets from the immortal Han Chung Li, also known as the Yuen F'ang Master. According to one version, when he was sixty-four years old, he visited the capital city of Ch'ang-an. At a wine shop there, he noticed an old man drinking wine and writing poetry on the walls. He was struck by the depth of Taoist sentiments expressed in one of the old man's poems, which went something like this:

> Sitting and dozing I always have a pot of wine at hand;
> My eyes don't wish to see the capital of the emperor;
> I am a lazy fellow who enjoys leisure;
> My name is not famous between heaven and earth.

Lu Tung Pin was so impressed that he approached the old man and asked who he was. The man revealed he was Master Yuen F'ang and invited Lu Tung Pin to go with him to the mountains and become his disciple. Lu Tung Pin was attracted by the idea but said nothing, for he actually had come to the capital hoping to be appointed to some official position. After a while the old master got up to cook some brown rice, but Lu Tung Pin felt a bit drowsy from the wine and leaned back on his pillow. In a moment, he fell asleep and began to dream. He dreamed he passed the official examinations in the highest place and married a daughter of the royal family. Then he became an important official and held a number of positions of great prestige and authority. After nearly forty years, he was promoted to the position of premier. But after ten years as premier, he became involved in a serious scandal. He was found guilty, condemned to exile, and separated from his family. Exiled to a remote, mountainous place, he found himself alone, caught in a blizzard, suffering a great deal, and sighing bitterly. Suddenly he awoke with a start. To his surprise, he found that Yuen F'ang's rice was not yet done cooking. The dream had such a powerful effect on him that he was convinced of the foolishness of all worldly ambition. He followed Yuen F'ang into the Ho Ling Mountains and became his disciple, learning from him the mysteries of alchemy and the elixir of everlasting life. It is said that before he was able to become immortal, he had to survive a series of ten temptations arranged by the magic of his master in order to test him. After he successfully overcame these, he too was given supernatural powers and also a magic sword, with which he traveled throughout China, slaying monsters and getting rid of all kinds of evils.

A humorous episode in modern Chinese history illustrates how the cult of Lu Tung Pin has persisted as an important aspect of folk culture and that it was influential not only among the illiterate peasants but the educated elite as well. In 1936, a military strongman and political leader in Kwangtung Province planned to challenge the authority of the central Chinese government in Nanking. Just before the challenge was about to break out as an open rebellion, he began to doubt whether it would be successful. His doubts led him to ask his brother to consult Lu Tung Pin by Chi divination. His brother did so and obtained the characters: Chi Pu K'o Shih, which may be translated as "Don't lose the opportunity." Chen Chi T'ang was delighted by what he took to be a highly favorable prediction and declared war on the central government. However, the character "chi," which means "opportunity," also has the meaning "airplanes." As it turned out, as soon as war was declared, Chen Chi T'ang's air force deserted him and the pilots all flew their planes to airbases controlled by the Nanking government. When he lost control of his army shortly afterward, he was forced to surrender. This story is well known and often recounted. A written report of it in an article by Liu Chien Ch'un appeared in the periodical *Chuan Chi Wen Hsueh*.[11]

Another of the Eight Immortals, Chang Kuo, was born around the middle of the seventh century, although many accounts say that he originally lived in very ancient times, during the 3d millennium B.C. Unlike Lu Tung Pin, he never aspired to any official position but lived as a hermit on Chung T'iao Mountain in Shansi. Because of his great skill in necromancy, he was much sought after by the T'ang emperors T'ai Tsung and Kao Tsung, who kept inviting him to their courts so that they could witness his magic. But in classic Taoist style, Chang Kuo persisted in refusing to go. Finally, when the empress Wu Tse T'ien demanded his presence, he agreed to leave the mountains and travel to the capital. But no sooner did he arrive there than he suddenly dropped dead. Very soon his body began to decompose and be eaten by worms. But it was all a magic trick, for he was seen a short time later, alive and well, back in the mountains. He is often pictured riding a donkey, and it is said that the donkey is made of paper, capable of being folded up and stashed in a suitcase when it is not needed. Whenever Chang Kuo wishes to go somewhere in a hurry, he simply takes the paper donkey out of his bag and magically changes it into a real donkey—indeed a donkey with exceptional powers, for he is able to ride it a thousand miles in a day.

Another legend has it that Chang Kuo actually appeared at the court of the Emperor Hsuan Tsung in A.D. 723 and entertained the emperor with a number of magic tricks, including making himself invisible and bringing down birds from the sky simply by pointing at them. The emperor is said to have offered him the opportunity to marry an imperial maid of honor, but he refused. Chang Kuo may have been more interested to meet Emperor Hsuan Tsung than the others whose invitations he refused, but Hsuan Tsung, also known as the T'ang Ming Hwang Emperor, was of all the T'ang emperors the most serious in the study and practice of Taoism. His activities as a commentator on the Taoist classics and his organization of Taoism as an official state religion have been described in Chapter 3. If there was a single high point in the practice of Taoist magic and other techniques in all of Chinese history, it came during his reign. Many magicians came to his court and became famous because of their exploits there, including Lo Tze Fang, Shen T'ai Chieh, and Lo Kung Yuan. The last of these is said to have used his magic to enable the emperor to travel to the moon to visit the fair lady who lives in the Moon Palace. This event is commemorated each year on a traditional holiday that occurs in mid-autumn, known as the Festival of T'ang Ming Hwang's Voyage to the Moon Palace. Some years ago, this story became the basis of a very popular movie in Taiwan.

The unity of the T'ang empire began to suffer erosion after the rebellion led by the dissident general An Lu Shan in A.D. 755. The dynasty survived until 906, however, collapsing as a result of military weakness against barbarian invasions as well as disintegration of its prestige and authority. But only a few decades later, a revival of culture began under the Sung dynasty. The Sung capital was at Kaifeng from 960 until 1126, when it moved to Hangchow, reigning there until it fell to the Mongols in 1279. Earlier chapters have described some of the religious and philosophical developments of the Sung period, so it is not necessary here to put the practice of magic during this time into historical perspective. It is known that the cult magic of the Pa Hsien was actively practiced, and many of the legends associated with them originated, during the Sung dynasty. There were also Taoists who achieved immortality during the Sung period and became comparable cult figures, such as the so-called Seven Enlightened Masters, mentioned in Chapter 3. Another character who lived during this time is also worth mentioning here because he has recently become widely known as the inventor of T'ai Chi Ch'uan, a form of health exercise and martial arts increasingly popular in both China and the West. He was Chang San Feng, an enlightened Taoist, who is said to have lived for between 200 and 300 years and then become immortal. His physical prowess was phenomenal; he could travel a thousand miles in a day on foot, eat many bushels of rice in a single day, and then go for many months without eating at all. There are many folk legends about feats he performed by magic, and there are dozens of mountains in many different parts of China where he was believed to have meditated and taught students.

In recent years numerous books have appeared in which traditional magic beliefs and practices have been described, including those of China as well as other cultures. A particularly interesting perspective on magic in Chinese culture can be gotten from Joseph Needham's great work, *Science and Civilization in China*.[12] Other valuable information on Chinese magic can be found in the writings of John Blofeld.[13] Yet these accounts, like the earlier parts of this chapter, are mainly historical in their approach and take much of their material from sources of the fairly remote past.

What is less readily available to Western readers today is reliable information about the nature and extent of magic practices in recent Chinese culture. It is a fact that magic is a living part of Chinese tradition. Before the Communist revolution, belief in magic was widespread, and there were a number of famous Taoist magicians. Even today, the tradition survives on Taiwan. Although this book is not the place in which to attempt a systematic account of magic in twentieth-century China, a few anecdotes from my own experience can perhaps give some indication of the survival of the old traditions and the fate of magicians in recent history.

In 1936, when the Japanese armies occupied Nanking and Shanghai, I moved south to Ch'angsha in Hunan Province. Soon after I arrived there, I read a newspaper account of the execution of a popular magician named Chou Chung P'ing. He had been found guilty of using magic to steal money from the army, thus jeopardizing the war effort against the Japanese. After making some inquiries, I found out the details of what happened. The story is interesting for what it tells about the vivid belief in magic on the part of the people involved and also about the vulnerable position the magician found himself in as a result of insisting on following his usual customs.

It happened that a military supply officer among the troops stationed near the provincial capital at Ch'angsha lost a great deal of cash which was supposed to be used to pay the soldiers their wages. When he discovered that the money was lost, he became very worried, for he was well aware of the severe punishment he could suffer under the provisions of martial law. In his desperation, he followed the advice of some people who suggested he find the magician Chou Chung P'ing, who was called "Immortal" and was quite famous among the local people. For years he had practiced many kinds of tricks, including one in which he would find objects that had been lost by going down to the river and fishing for them with a hook and line. Although he used quite ordinary fishing tackle, his magic was such that he could usually manage to haul the lost object from the water, no matter what it might be. As payment for his services, he would customarily receive a percentage of the value of the objects he recovered. Chou was not a rich man, however, for he gambled incessantly and almost always lost money.

When the military officer came to him to ask his help in recovering a large sum of money, Chou Chung P'ing made his usual response: Of course he would be able to use his magic to recover the money; the only requirement would be that he get to keep half of it as payment for his services. As usual, the response did not represent any sort of rigid requirement, but only his initial negotiating position, and he soon indicated to the officer that he might be willing to perform the trick for a smaller percentage, as long as it was at least one-third of the missing sum. But the officer refused to negotiate, for he knew the money belonged to the army. If he paid Chou Chung P'ing any fee at all, he would not be able to raise the full amount he had lost and would be punished. So the negotiations broke down, the two men quarreled and fought, and the officer went away empty-handed.

Soon afterward he reported the loss of the money to Chang Chih Chung, the governor and military commander of Hunan. Instead of telling the truth about how it was lost, he told the governor that Chou Chung P'ing had used his magic to steal the payroll. Now, the magician Chou was well known to the governor, who had heard about his magic tricks and was also aware of his gambling habits. Rumors had been going around for some time to the effect that he got the money to pay his gambling debts by magic. In fact, Chang Chih Chung had become convinced that these rumors and other superstitions associated with his activities were confusing the people and interfering with the government's efforts in the war against the

Japanese. Therefore, Chang Chih Chung seized the opportunity presented by the officer's accusations and had the magician executed. Thus, although he was innocent of the charges, Chou Chung P'ing's life came to an unfortunate end. He had been a genuine magician, however, and could accomplish really astonishing tricks, and so his fame continued long after his death.

Years later I met a Hunanese native who told me about an experience he had once had in Wuhan city, several hundred miles from Ch'angsha. He had gambled and drunk with a group of people from Hunan, one of whom was Chou Chung P'ing. During the course of the evening someone remarked, rather wistfully, about how nice it would be if they could all go to the T'ien Hsin Ko (Heavenly Heart Pavilion), an exquisite restaurant back in their home town of Ch'angsha. Of course that was impossible, but they were all Hunanese and each felt a certain amount of homesickness, which the remark aptly evoked.

But Chou Chung P'ing wouldn't let it go at that. He went around making people develop their fantasies in great detail, asking each what particular dish he would order from the restaurant. Then he withdrew to the next room for about twenty minutes. When he returned, he brought with him portions of all the dishes the various people had mentioned, all freshly prepared and piping hot. After the food was tasted, everyone agreed in amazement that they knew of nowhere in the world that such delicious food could be enjoyed except in the T'ien Hsin Ko in Ch'angsha. But as they were eating with great gusto, some people began to joke about the "magic trick" they had witnessed, laughingly suggesting that perhaps Chou Chung P'ing kept a Hunanese cook hidden in a closet for just such occasions, and so on. Before long the meal was finished, and the people began to examine the bowls and platters on which it had been served. On each one they found the characters T'ien Hsin Ko clearly painted.

Chou Chung P'ing's addiction to gambling was well known, and many people were puzzled by the fact that he always seemed to lose. "Since you are so highly accomplished in the arts of magic," he was asked, "why can't you use the magic to bring it about that you win more often?" In reply, he pointed out that he was a social gambler who got most of his enjoyment from playing games with people. "If I really used magic and won all the time," he said, "no one would be willing to play with me."

Another story about Chou Chung P'ing may be partly fiction, or at least its factual content is difficult to judge. It is said that some time before the Sino-Japanese war, a foreign naval vessel was anchored in the Hsiang River near Ch'angsha. One day the captain of the vessel called on a local government official, announced that one of the ship's cannons was missing, and angrily demanded that the force of the Chinese government be used to help get it back. The official was incredulous and pointed out to the captain the absurdity of his story. "How could you lose a cannon?" he asked. "It is a very heavy object floating on a heavily guarded boat in the middle of the river. There is no conceivable way for the people to have gotten it. Perhaps you had better go back and check to see if it is really lost." After the foreign captain left in embarrassment, the official thought to himself about the strangeness of the affair. It simply did not make sense. Some time later, a rumor began to go around that Chou Chung P'ing had used magic to make the foreigners' cannon disappear. Chou was once asked about it, but he simply smiled and neither admitted nor denied it.

Many people who heard about or even witnessed the feats of magicians such as Chou Chung P'ing did not really appreciate the kind of effort and commitment required to learn these arts. It was easy to be misled by the appearance of the magicians, who were usually bizarre-looking and often were homeless beggars who seemed to live quite dissolute lives. Actually, however, to be able to control the powers of magic it is necessary to develop a very intense level of mental concentration for which rigorous discipline and unceasing practice are essential. The masters may have looked like carefree idlers to the casual observer; indeed, to affect such a style was in the authentic Taoist tradition. But anyone who could manage to observe them more carefully discovered that they engaged in daily rituals— such as facing the sun at dawn, noon, and dusk; swallowing the rays of the sun; and reciting the secret words of magic sayings.

It would be quite impossible to explain in written form just how their magic spells worked and equally impossible to give a realistic account of the process by which one might learn to become a magician. It is certainly true that no one ever really learned magic from a book. To be initiated into these arts, it is necessary to study with a master personally for a long period of time. And even to become a student of such a master was always enormously difficult, for these strange characters were usually quite unapproachable. Even if one were deemed a worthy candidate for their instruction, one had to be prepared to make considerable sacrifices to indicate one's seriousness and sincerity. Students would always be required to take an oath that they would never reveal the words of magic spells or other information to anyone. Most masters would also require the prospective student to swear never to steal from or take advantage of people by the use of magic. In addition, it was generally required that as a price for learning the magic secrets, one had to agree to give up either riches, family, or home for life. That is, a magician had to make a commitment either to become a poor beggar, never to marry and have descendants, or to become a homeless wanderer. Most became wanderers who traveled aimlessly about the countryside. At New Year's time, when all the people traditionally went to their homes to celebrate the holiday, these strange Taoists would often stay in temples, where they were welcome, since they had no homes of their own to go to.

NOTES

1. See ch. 5, p. 43.
2. See ch. 9.
3. See especially *The Shu Ching or Book of Historical Documents*, trans. James Legge, in *The Chinese Classics (CC)*, Hong Kong, 1960, vol. 5, part 2, book 1, pp. 92–150.
4. *CC*, vol. 2, p. 279.
5. *Chuang Tzu*, ch. 6; see *The Texts of Taoism (TT)*, trans. James Legge, Oxford University Press, 1891, vol. 2, pp. 237–38.
6. *Chuang Tzu*, ch. 1; *TT*, pp. 168–69.
7. Reprinted in *The Collected Writings of Liu Ch'ien Ch'un*, Taipei, 1966, vol. 3, pp. 33–47.
8. Joseph Needham, *Science and Civilization in China*, Cambridge University Press, 1956, vol. 2, p. 157.
9. To be discussed in ch. 10.

10. See *The Secret of the Golden Flower: A Chinese Book of Life*, trans. Cary F. Baynes from the German version by Richard Wilhelm and C.G. Jung; London: Kegan Paul, 1931.

11. Reprinted in *Collected Writings of Liu Ch'ien Ch'un, op. cit.*, p. 81.

12. See especially vol. 2, p. 157.

13. John Blofeld, *The Secret and Sublime: Taoist Mysteries and Magic*, New York: Dutton, 1973.

chapter 8
TAOiSM ANd MEditation

The Chinese term for meditation is *Ching Tsuo,* which means literally "sitting peacefully." Of all the techniques whose development in China has been associated with Taoism, it is properly regarded as most central. For the individual striving to realize the personal salvation envisioned by the Taoist religion, the practice of meditation has always been necessary, whether complemented by other practices such as alchemy and magic or not. Yet to describe its importance strictly from a Taoist point of view is to offer too narrow a picture of the significance of meditation in Chinese culture. As a religious activity, it has an important role in all forms of religion known in traditional China, Buddhists and Moslems being just as devoted to its practice as Taoists. Moreover, the practice of meditation has been developed not only by religions, but by political and military organizations as well, such as the Yi Ho Tu'an and the Red Spear Association, mentioned in Chapter 6. It has long been recognized by the Chinese that, in order to attain a high level of excellence in active skills such as martial arts or magic, it is essential to complement the periods of movement in practicing these techniques with periods of quiet meditation. This insight comes directly from the concept of Yin and Yang, perhaps the most widely applicable principle in Chinese thought. Indeed, it can be extended to apply not only to the process of learning refined skills but also to the attainment of health and success in everyday life. Accordingly, the practice of meditation in traditional China was not limited to an elite minority but was a custom widespread among the people, motivated largely by a desire for its health benefits, and especially common among the elderly. In modern times, with the growth of the industrialized urban society in which people must live and work at a fast pace, often under great pressure, the importance of being able to sit quietly and meditate for a while each day has greatly increased. Such a practice has a purifying effect on the mind not unlike that which can be seen in a quiet puddle after a rain, when the mud and other impurities have a chance to settle out, leaving the water clean and clear. As such, it offers a way toward inner peace and preservation of sanity that answers to a significant social need throughout the world today.

In this chapter, the discussion will be mainly limited to the subject of Taoist meditation, including the practices that originated in China during early antiquity, the theories underlying these practices set forth in the Taoist classics of Lao Tzu and Chuang Tzu, and the development of this tradition in later times after Taoism emerged as a religion. Because of the organizational and spatial limits of this book, it is not possible to present here a thorough description of these meditation techniques sufficient to give the reader a clear idea of how to go about practicing them; we must be content to introduce the basic ideas and to provide information about the history of the techniques and their influence in Chinese society. Interested readers will find a more instructional approach to the subject in some of my other writings, both past and forthcoming.[1]

The immediate aim of meditation is to make the mind peaceful by emptying it of desires and emotions. Thus it is largely a process of "sitting and forgetting." The process is often described as "nourishing the vital spirit"[2] or "cultivating the mind," but these metaphors are apt to be misleading unless one is aware of what is involved in the Chinese concept of the spiritual dimension of human life. The word most properly translated as "spirit" or "mind" is *shen*. Each person is believed to have a *shen* located within his or her body, and it is the center of all emotions, thoughts, intentions, and other mental activities and dispositions. The *shen* is not the sole spiritual aspect of the person, however, for there are in addition the *ch'i* and the *ching*. The term *ch'i* is commonly translated as "vitality" but also can be rendered as "breath." It is regarded as a kind of life energy that pervades the body and even its surrounding space, an energy that supports movement and all the activities of daily life. It is also identified with the breath, since its function of invigorating and cleansing the tissues throughout the body is accomplished by its circulation through the "psychic channels," which is coordinated with the breathing cycle. In this connection it should be mentioned that for the Chinese, the concept of "breathing" has since ancient times involved not merely the inhalation and exhalation of gases to and from the lungs, but the function of the circulatory system to bring nourishment to and waste products from the cells throughout the body. A comparable understanding of the process of respiration was not achieved in the West until much more recent times. The tendency of the Chinese to describe the process in spiritual terms, using the concept of *ch'i,* may be partly attributed to the recognition that vigor and energy as manifest in a person's daily activities are functions of emotional as well as physical factors, but it is also true that gases and vapors have always been regarded by the Chinese more as spiritual presences than as material substances. (For the ancient Greeks, air was one of the four basic material elements of the universe. By contrast, the five elements of the Chinese tradition include wood and metal, but not air.) Perhaps the most important reason underlying the Chinese description of the breath as a spiritual entity, however, arises from the direct experience of the practice of meditation, as we will see below.

The *ching* is closely related to the other spiritual components, for it is regarded as the source of both *ch'i* and *shen*. As an English translation, the term "sexual energy" is appropriate, for *ching* is most accurately thought of as a mental aspect present in sperm and egg. Occasionally one sees it translated as "semen," but this is too limited, for *ching* is present in both male and female. An important use of this form of energy occurs in the process of reproduction, for the power of male and female to create new life by the combining of their sexual fluids is a result of the *ching* present in these fluids. This is not its only purpose, however, for the Taoist practice of meditation is based on the idea that the *ching* can be transformed into *ch'i* through a process of refinement and purification occurring within the body. By continuing the refinement, in fact, the *ch'i* can be further transformed until it becomes *shen*. Thus, the three spiritual components—mind, vitality, and sexual energy—while distinct in their function and able to be perceived separately, are ultimately thought of as three different aspects of a single unity, which can be transformed from one to another through the practice of meditation.

It is worth emphasizing that the transformation of *ching* into *ch'i* and finally into *shen* is regarded as a natural process, not artificially produced through meditation. The function of meditation is simply to manage or govern this natural process so that it will occur more efficiently and result in greater benefits of health and longevity for those who practice it. The intuitive basis of this belief can be explained rather simply. Sexual energy is greatest during youth, when it is produced in large quantities through the natural functioning of the reproductive organs. During this same period of life, people manifestly possess greater strength and vigor than at any other time. Furthermore, it is generally observed that gains and losses of vital energy affect not only physical but mental capabilities as well. The powers of concentration, creative thought, and accurate memory often deteriorate when people lose vital energy through illness, for example, and may be restored when they become well again. Thus the idea that certain forms of spiritual energy essential for life may be produced by the transformation of others comes about as a natural explanation for phenomena that can be observed in the daily lives of almost everyone. In addition, this same idea can be used to describe the process of aging and the accompanying deterioration of physical and mental powers experienced by most people. For it is usual that young people, whose *ching* is very great, have enormous enthusiasm for sexual activities. No doubt these activities have considerable value, since among other things they result in the creation of the next generation of human life. But there is also no doubt that in the course of such activities, a great deal of sexual energy is spent, passing out of the body as part of the reproductive process. Thus it is no longer available to be transformed into vital energy or spirit. After a relatively short time, the body ceases to create *ching* in large amounts, and so losses of vital energy cannot so easily be restored. Eventually it is no longer produced at all, after which loss of vitality and spirit are inevitable, resulting in deterioration and death. With reference to this way of looking at the phenomenon of aging, Taoist meditation can be described as essentially a method of reversing the direction of the process so that spiritual energy is conserved and refined instead of being lost. Rather than allowing *ching* to be spent in sexual activities, the Taoist retains it within the body and allows it to be gradually purified into *ch'i* and *shen,* which can then be saved up in concentrated form to be used to sustain life and preserve the vigor of youth for an indefinite period of time. The process of purification is in two stages. In the first, the *ching* is circulated through the abdominal cavity and combined with the elements present in the five inner organs. This is called the Lesser Heavenly Circulation.

After it is repeated very many times, a change occurs so that the *ching* is transformed into *ch'i.* In the form of *ch'i,* the energy can be further refined in the second stage of the purification process, in which the *ch'i* is circulated through a network of psychic channels within the body. To enable this circulatory movement of the *ch'i* to occur, it is heated within the abdomen until it is sent downward to the base of the spine. From there it can rise up the spinal column to the crown of the head, then down the forehead to the mouth, through the throat and down the front of the body to the abdomen, whence another cycle can begin. This is called the Greater Heavenly Circulation. There are also other cyclic pathways through which the *ch'i* can be circulated to other parts of the body, even to the fingertips and the soles of the feet.

The circulations of spiritual energy involved in these purification processes are accomplished by means of mental concentration in the practice of meditation. The beginner in the practice must learn consciously to guide the flow of energy and to coordinate it with the slow rhythm of inhalations and exhalations in deep breathing. It is possible to do this in a sitting posture, but it can also be done while standing, and various kinds of limb movements have been found to be helpful in leading the *ch'i* through the psychic channels. At a more advanced level, the meditator experiences the spontaneous circulation of the *ch'i* without conscious effort, in some cases accompanied by powerful sensations. The abdomen becomes hot as fire, the *ch'i* rushes to the spine like steam. As it rises up the spine, it becomes more and more rarified, until it reaches the head (the room of *shen*) where it produces a sensation of great emptiness and peace. As this emptiness spreads downward, it condenses in the form of saliva, which appears in the rear of the mouth, is swallowed, and goes down to the abdomen where it is heated, starting the cycle over again. Occasionally, these sensations are accompanied by involuntary movements of the limbs.

The circulation of spiritual energy through the body during meditation has been described in Taoist writings and spoken tradition by means of various metaphors. One of the principal ones is the analogy of plant growth throughout the year. This is often expressed with the use of the *I Ching* symbols, for the twelve "psychic centers" through which the energy flows during the Greater Heavenly Circulation are represented by the twelve hexagrams known as the "Waxing and Waning of Yin and Yang." The same set of hexagrams is used to represent the twelve months of the year, the progression from one to the other symbolizing the various stages in the growth of grain, beginning with the seed which sprouts, grows up, flowers, produces fruits which ripen and are purified to obtain seeds for next year, as well as the harvest that can be used as nourishment for human life. In an analogous way, the increase and decrease in the pattern of Yin and Yang lines in these twelve hexagrams also symbolize the growth of spiritual energy, beginning with the seed *(ching)* which develops into *ch'i,* becomes more spiritually refined while moving up the spine, and after reaching its high point in the room of *shen,* is distilled into liquid form as saliva, which becomes *ching* in the abdomen, producing the seed for the next cycle.

Other metaphors were also developed in order to describe this process. A rather esoteric one that appears in later Taoist writings compares the process with the methods of refinement used by alchemists in their efforts to turn ordinary substances into an "elixir of immortality," a potion that could produce everlasting youth. In fact, the terminology of alchemy and meditation evolved along parallel lines, to the extent that certain old Taoist treatises can be read either as referring to chemical processes that could be carried out in the alchemist's laboratory or to spiritual processes that could take place within the meditator's body. The *I Ching* symbolism was also interpreted so as to express this analogy, for the twelve hexagrams representing the twelve psychic centers along the Greater Heavenly Circulation also represent twelve flasks into and out of which the elixir passes during the alchemical refinement process.

The description of meditation in terms of the concepts of *shen, ch'i* and *ching* evolved over a period of many centuries during which the practice of meditation gradually became more highly developed. The origin of this practice in China occurred in what must be considered prehistoric times. The Emperor Hwang Ti's visit to the immortal Kuang Ch'eng Tzu on K'ung-tung Mountain, mentioned in Chapter 1, is traditionally believed to have occurred around 2680 B.C. Yet according to Chuang Tzu's account, the immortal sage had already achieved a very advanced level in the practice. In his advice to Hwang Ti, however, he spoke neither of controlling the breath, nor of various forms of spiritual energy. Instead, his main emphasis is to be found in the following quotation: "Let there be no looking, no listening. Wrap your spirit [*shen*] in stillness; then your body will become correct. You must remain quiet and empty. Do not overwork your body; do not allow your vitality to become agitated. Then you will live long."[3] This passage is typical of the ideas about meditation predominant in China prior to the Han period. The practice of peaceful sitting was mainly regarded as a way of cultivating the spirit *(shen)* by emptying it of all thoughts and desires. This was certainly the view emphasized by Lao Tzu, in aphorisms such as the beginning of the sixteenth chapter of the *Tao Te Ching:* "The condition of emptiness should be attained to the utmost degree, and that of quiescence maintained with constant vigor."[4] Another chapter of Lao Tzu's classic speaks of "giving undivided attention to the breath [vitality] and bringing it to the utmost degree of pliancy" (Chapter 10). But this is actually quite simple, merely hinting at what writers in later centuries would make their main emphasis. By comparison, the idea of achieving peace and quiet by emptying the mind of thoughts is much more closely connected with the main philosophical themes developed throughout Lao Tzu's writings.

An interesting fact not often noticed by modern writers is that the practice of sitting quietly and emptying the mind is advocated not only in the Taoist classics, but also in the ancient writings of the Confucianist school. It is most explicit in the writings of Meng Tzu, such as in the remark, "For nourishing the spirit *shen,* nothing is better than emptying it of desires."[5]

This may be taken as one of many indications that Meng Tzu was influenced by Taoist ideas; but on the other hand, it may also suggest that the basic idea of sitting peacefully to quiet the mind was not originally a Taoist invention but a cultural practice that predated the development of Taoist and Confucianist ideologies and whose value was recognized by both.

The writings of Chuang Tzu, which date from roughly the same time as those of Meng Tzu, contain much greater detail on the subject of meditation than any other ancient sources. The practice of sitting quietly and forgetting is mentioned many times by Chuang Tzu, in passages that characterize the ideal of emptying the mind in quite radical terms. For example, he tells of a conversation between Confucius and Yen Hui, in which the latter describes his "improvement" as not merely a process of forgetting about morals and propriety, or ceremonies and music, but a much more fundamental renunciation of the common ways of thought and experience: "My connection with my body and its parts is dissolved. Seeing and hearing are discarded. Thus leaving my material form, and quitting all my knowledge, I become one with the Great Void [Tao]. This I call sitting and forgetting all things."[6] One who achieves this kind of emptiness can sit awake without thinking, can sleep without dreaming, and no longer even cares about the difference between life and death. Such was the way of the "True Men of Old," according to Chuang Tzu.

But certain other parts of Chuang Tzu's writings also describe controlling the breath, indicating that such a practice is closely associated with the attainment of the spiritual aims of meditation. "The respiration of ordinary people is from their throats," says another passage in the same chapter just quoted, "but the True Men of Old breathed from their heels." Another passage apparently refers to the movement of the *ch'i* up the spinal column (*Tu Mo*), calling the cultivation of such a practice "the regular way to preserve the body, maintain life..., and complete our term of years."[7] Perhaps the most often quoted passage from the *Chuang Tzu* pertaining to this subject is in Chapter 15, which describes the practices of "inhaling and exhaling the breath from the different inner organs, expelling the old breath and taking in new, moving like a bear, and stretching the neck like a bird." But Chuang Tzu's attitude toward such practices does not appear to be one of wholehearted approval, for the context places them on a par with various other "know-hows" which tend to agitate and disturb the mind, and the passage continues:

> All this simply shows a desire for longevity...But as to those...who attain to longevity without the management of the breath, who forget all things and yet possess all things, whose quietude is unlimited...such men pursue the Tao of heaven and earth, and display the characteristics of the sages.[8]

Some historians, especially Western Sinologists who have tried to make a sharp distinction between the so-called philosophical aspects of Taoism and the practices related to the attainment of immortality, which became predominant in later Taoism, have interpreted these statements as evidence that Chuang Tzu, whom they regard as among the foremost of the philosophical Taoists, did not advocate the practice of meditation techniques.

A more reasonable interpretation does not warrant this conclusion, however. It is quite likely that Chuang Tzu, well aware that these techniques had been deeply rooted in the tradition from which his philosophy evolved for centuries, nevertheless thought it worth emphasizing that they are correctly regarded as only means toward the attainment of the central goal of meditation: an empty and peaceful mind, means that may be helpful, but are neither necessary nor sufficient. Too much emphasis on the techniques may hinder success by making one lose sight of what is of real value and may be genuinely harmful to mental as well as physical health. Chinese lore includes many stories of people who, in spite of great intelligence and a high level of advancement in meditation techniques, have ultimately found in them a source not of inner peace, but of madness.

An example can be found in the great Chinese novel, *The Dream of the Red Chamber (Hung Lo Meng)*, in which such a fate befalls one of the characters, a beautiful maiden named Miou Yu, who became a Buddhist nun. She was highly intelligent and clever, unusually inclined to spiritual reflection, and reached a profound level of understanding of the theory of Ch'an (Zen) meditation. Moreover, she lived under conditions ideal for the successful practice of meditation, for she spent nearly all her time in the temple where she lived, attended by several servants, and had neither work nor other responsibilities to distract her. Yet in spite of all these advantages, she did not achieve success, but instead developed mental and emotional problems that made her very unhappy. Unfortunately, such occurrences are not only to be found in fiction. I am acquainted with a man, the brother of one of my students, who has been in a mental hospital for several years after he got into trouble through the intense practice of meditation techniques which he had traveled to India in order to learn. He is still hospitalized in Philadelphia today. It is the danger of just such occurrences that Chuang Tzu warns against in the passage quoted above.

To appreciate fully the historical significance of Chuang Tzu's writings on meditation, it must be kept in mind that they were written centuries before there was any significant cultural contact between China and India. Thus the ideas found in them should be regarded as records of indigenous Chinese practices not the imitation of Indian ones. Of course the Indian yoga tradition did eventually have quite an influence on Taoist religion, but this was not significant until much later. By that time the concepts involved in meditation had already been highly developed by the Chinese. Even the concept of the relationship between mind *(shen)* and breath *(ch'i)* can be seen in the early Chinese writings. Meng Tzu, for example, makes a clear distinction between these two spiritual aspects but holds that the mind *(shen)* is the superior, for it has the power to control the *ch'i*.[9]

The writers of the ancient classics were not at all specialized in their interest in the theory of meditation, of course. It was but one of a great many topics they discussed, and their teachings concerning it sometimes even escape the notice of careful readers, if they are not sufficiently familiar with the meditation practices themselves. The earliest specialized treatise entirely devoted to the theory of meditation still extant is the famous *Ts'an T'ung Ch'i* (Book of the Kinship of the Three), which first appeared around A.D. 142. Written by Wei Po-yang during the Eastern Han dynasty, it can be considered the bible of Taoist meditation; for though a vast number of other books on Taoist meditation were produced during the succeeding centuries, they mainly follow and elaborate upon Wei Po-yang's ideas. These ideas are solidly based on the traditional philosophy of Yin and Yang found in the *I Ching*. Using both the trigram and hexagram symbols as well as material from the *Ta Chuan* (The Great Treatise), Wei Po-yang developed a description according to which processes occurring within the body during meditation are governed by the same fundamental forces that control the universe on the largest scale. Joseph Needham has called the *Ts'an T'ung Ch'i* the first book on alchemy in Chinese (and, indeed, in any other) history.[10] To be properly understood, this remark should be considered in the context of the close connection between alchemy and meditation we have already mentioned. In fact, it can be truly said that the Chinese concept of alchemy includes that of meditation, for it refers to the combination of many different elements together to create the "elixir of immortality." Such a combination can occur within the body, to form an "inner elixir," or it can occur outside the body to form an "outer elixir," in the form of either a pill to be eaten or a liquor to be drunk. The former can be carried out through the methods of meditation, the latter through methods of combining herbal and mineral substances, which will be further described in the next chapter. Both methods can be considered "alchemy," and both are simultaneously described in Wei Po-yang's treatise.

The *Ts'an T'ung Ch'i* influenced all later Chinese thought on the subject of meditation, but its prestige and authority became most significant during the Sung dynasty, when it was highly admired by the neo-Confucianist philosophers. Chu Hsi, the so-called Third Sage of Confucianism, even composed a commentary on it. But in spite of its prestige and influence, the book itself is extremely difficult to understand. One reason is that it relies so much on the *I Ching*, itself notoriously obscure due to its great antiquity and philosophical depth. In addition, Wei Po-yang made extensive use of technical terminology of the Taoist tradition, and the precise meaning of many characters is nearly impenetrable—even Chu Hsi's commentary is often of very little help. Actually, however, it is not impossible to understand the wisdom contained in the *Ts'an T'ung Ch'i*. Provided that one possesses sufficient knowledge of Taoism and the *I Ching*, such understanding can be achieved by patiently reading the book over and over again. It is essential that each person who wishes to understand must do this for himself; it is not enough to read commentaries or accounts of what others may think the book means. It is an example that illustrates the point of Lao Tzu's saying: "The *Tao* that can be spoken of is not the real *Tao*." For Westerners who cannot read the *Ts'an T'ung Ch'i* in the original Chinese, a first-hand understanding of it is even more difficult to experience, of course, but an English translation, which appeared in 1932,[11] may give a glimpse of what this might be like.

The introduction into China of ideas and customs that originated in India, especially those of the Buddhist religion, has been described in earlier chapters. As we indicated, their influence began during the Han dynasty and reached a high point between the third and seventh centuries A.D. Its impact on Chinese culture was felt in many ways, but especially in the realm of religion, where the response to Buddhism led to the evolution of Taoist religion. There can be no doubt that an important aspect of Buddhist influence had to do with the theory and practice of meditation, for this practice was the principal function through which Buddhists attempted to achieve their religious goals. It is inaccurate, however, to suggest that Buddhist theories and techniques were simply copied by the Taoists.

In the first place, as we have already mentioned, the theory and practice of meditation existed in China long before the Buddhists first arrived. Furthermore, there are subtle but important differences between Buddhist and Taoist meditation, differences that pertain both to the conception of the role of meditation in achieving salvation and to the techniques themselves. The Buddhists tend to regard meditation exclusively in spiritual terms. To put it very simply, the idea is that by making the mind quiet, the meditator grows in wisdom and eventually becomes "enlightened." The aim is to make the spirit more and more independent of the body, so that it can be reincarnated in more favorable circumstances in its next life, or, at the highest level, escape the cycle of reincarnation entirely and become an enlightened Buddha, dwelling in a blissful place.[12] As a result, the concepts and methods of the Buddhist tradition emphasize spiritual growth, even to the extent of neglecting the physical health of the meditator entirely. The Taoists, on the other hand, think of meditation in terms of a peculiar synthesis between mind and body that could be achieved by nourishing both together. Although the Taoist classics emphasize spiritual growth above all, the practical tradition of meditation makes it clear that the spirit should be nourished by physical techniques as well.

The integration of spiritual and physical development that characterizes the Taoist approach can be seen vividly in another image used in some Taoist writings to describe the meditator's progress—the image of the Immortal Fetus. The basic idea is that after continually practicing the circulation of the vital energy through the psychic channels for a long time, the meditator begins to develop within his body an immortal spiritual embryo. Through a period of further practice, the embryo develops and becomes more mature, until it finally emerges from the body in a process analogous to the birth of a baby, except that it comes out of the top of the meditator's head, where the so-called Heavenly Gate is located. This must be understood as a metaphorical way of describing a spiritual process, of course no actual physical birth is envisioned. There are, however, physical experiences intimately connected with this process that resemble those of an expectant mother. The body of the meditator is essential to the successful outcome, and if it should become sick or die during the gestation period, the fetus would perish, and immortality would not be attained. So the practices of the meditator are regarded as ways of nourishing the body as well as the spirit and, like the prenatal health practices of the expectant mother, necessary to ensure the birth of a healthy baby.

The ideas about the Immortal Fetus and its growth within the body of the meditator evidently had a role in the Taoist meditation tradition even in Lao Tzu's time, for the tenth chapter of the *Tao Te*

Ching speaks of "opening and shutting the Heavenly Gate like a female." This reference occurs within one of the most difficult passages in Lao Tzu's writings, and it has often been misunderstood by translators. James Legge, for example, identifies "the gates of heaven" as "a Taoistic phrase for the nostrils as the organ of the breath,"[13] citing a Chinese commentary as his source. This is mistaken, however, for the Heavenly Gate is actually on the crown of the head, where the meditator develops a soft area similar to that on the head of a young infant. The opening of the crown of the head in this way is described in great detail in more recent treatises on meditation techniques and experiences.[14]

By the time of the T'ang dynasty, Buddhism so pervaded Chinese life that its ideas and practices tended to be thoroughly blended together with those of Taoism. The area of meditation was no exception to this tendency, and it was very common during and after this period for people to practice techniques of Taoist origin while at the same time thinking of themselves as striving for salvation in terms of Buddhist ideas. Nevertheless, an awareness of the difference in emphasis between Taoism and Buddhism remained in the Chinese cultural tradition. A story illustrating the difference can be found in the "Record of Buddhist and Taoist Immortals," which dates from the Sung dynasty period. The story concerns the enlightened Taoist master Chang Tze Yang, considered one of the five masters of the Southern School of Taoism. He was talking one day with a good friend who was a Buddhist monk, and they both thought of how it was then the season when there was a spectacular blooming of the Chung Hwa flowers, but these grew only at Yang Chou, a place some hundreds of *li* distant from them. Later, while they meditated together in the same room, both of their spirits traveled to Yang Chou and they saw the flowers. After they returned, they both described the scene there, so that there was no doubt that they had both been present. But Chang Tze Yang then reached up his sleeve and produced a fresh Chung Hwa flower. The point, of course, is that both he and the Buddhist monk were able to achieve the remarkable feat of transporting their spirits hundreds of li distant, but Chang Tze Yang, because of his Taoist practices, was able to achieve a physical as well as spiritual presence in the distant place, while the Buddhist could not. The later history of the evolution of Taoist meditation becomes increasingly complex. A vast variety of different methods and ways of thinking about meditation developed, and it is in some cases quite difficult to perceive how they relate to the teachings of the ancient tradition. Some schools aimed not at emptying the mind but at inducing gods to dwell within it, and their practices involved the worship of the moon, stars, and other Taoist deities. For example, the massive seven-volume treatise entitled *Yuen Chi Ch'i Ch'ien*, which dates from the Sung period, gives a detailed account of the particular gods and goddesses governing each part of the body, and even describes their appearance, specifying colors and types of clothing associated with each of them. Other schools kept more closely to the original Taoist methods and produced writings that give a more accurate picture of the practices of ancient times. During the eighteenth century, Liu Kwa Yang, a Buddhist monk wishing to achieve immortality, became a student of the renowned Taoist master Wu Ch'ung Hsu. He was remarkably successful in the practice of meditation and is believed to have finally become immortal. He wrote a book, *Huei Ming Ching*, which is an outstanding example of a successful blend of Taoism and Buddhism and contains a very accurate description of authentic Taoist traditional methods. It was one of Liu Kwa Yang's students who taught the Taoist master Chao Pi Chen, born in 1860, whose treatise *Hsin Ming Fa Chueh Ming Chih* has recently been translated into English under the title *Taoist Yoga*.[15] This book contains a rather detailed description of methods we have mentioned in this chapter, including the ideas of the formation and egress of the Immortal Fetus, as well as the techniques of purifying and refining the *ching* and *ch'i*.

A notorious source of confusion among students of Chinese cultural history has to do with the attitude toward sexuality and sexual activities which underlies the Taoist meditation tradition. Earlier in the chapter, we described Taoist meditation as essentially involving the practice of storing the sexual energy *(ching)* which is embodied in the sexual fluids (sperm in the male, menstrual fluid in the female), so that it can be refined into more concentrated forms of spiritual energy. Regarding the question of how to accomplish this, however, there seem to be two quite distinct schools of thought. One school holds that in order to prevent the *ching* from being spent, the meditator should abstain from sexual intercourse and should remain in solitude, gradually accumulating more and more energy until the Immortal Fetus is formed. The teaching to be found in the book *Taoist Yoga*, mentioned above, exemplifies this approach. Another school, however, teaches a number of techniques of sexual intercourse which male and female can practice together, enabling both to achieve more rapid advancement toward the aims of meditation than is possible for a single person to achieve by himself. Known as *shuang hsiu* ("double" or "cooperative" meditation), such methods are based on the great rhythm of nature, in which the opposing forces of Yin and Yang continually nourish one another. They have been practiced since ancient times, and they are known to have been highly successful in some cases. For example, the "Seven Enlightened Masters" of the Sung dynasty included both Ma Tan Yang and his wife Sun Pu Erh Niang, who achieved immortality together through the practice of such techniques.

The apparent conflict between these two schools of Taoist meditation has confused many people, leading them to wonder which is correct and which mistaken. Actually, however, there is not such a genuine conflict here as is sometimes thought. A great deal of misunderstanding has resulted from highly misleading ways of describing the sexual techniques. Such techniques, quite naturally, have always been a subject of great interest to many people, even to those who possessed only the most vague awareness of Taoist meditation. Hundreds of books about them have been written in China, and recent years have seen a number of them translated into Western languages.[16] Although some have become very popular, however, most have been based on a merely theoretical knowledge of the subject rather than on practical experience and fail to give an accurate impression of how difficult it is to really practice these methods.

According to authentic teachings, the techniques of sexual intercourse are intended to prevent the emission of sperm from the male as well as to stop the menstrual cycle of the female. The relationship between the partners can be thought of as somewhat analogous to a business partnership, in which the purpose is to make a profit without either of the partners losing any of the capital they have invested. Furthermore, the partners must practice the techniques very regularly, at certain prescribed times each day, and in a prescribed manner over a long period of time in order to achieve the beneficial effects. The process is similar to the care and nourishment of a plant, which needs just the right amount of water and sunlight on a regular schedule. If it is allowed to dry up for many days and then flooded with gallons of water, of course it will not survive. In view of the rigorous demands of such a regular practice, it is obvious that it can be accomplished successfully only in a relationship between a man and a woman that is characterized by a permanent commitment to each other and a serious devotion to the practice of meditation on both sides. Since genuine relationships of this kind are so rare, it is fair to say that the solitary meditation techniques, for all their rigorous asceticism, are an easier way to achieve the aims of meditation. It is certainly the case that those who suggest that such aims can be achieved by a life of frivolous sexual adventure are frauds and charlatans.

The necessity for practical experience of Taoist meditation methods in order to understand them correctly can hardly be overemphasized. Even highly qualified and well-meaning authors tend to become confused when they discuss matters that go beyond their own personal knowledge. For instance, Joseph Needham, who in addition to his great work as a student of Chinese cultural history is renowned as a biochemist, an expert in embryology as well as a practicing physician, devotes a section in his chapter on Taoism to a discussion of sexual techniques.[17] Describing the method of restricting the emission of the sperm during intercourse so that its essence can be made to ascend up the spinal column to the brain, rejuvenating the upper parts of the body, he points out that this is based on a belief that is physiologically mistaken. Actually, he says, the method merely diverts the seminal secretion into the bladder, whence it is later voided with the excreted urine. The trouble with this account, however, is that it fails to consider the step in the process whereby the *ching* is purified to become *ch'i*. Of course the *ching* cannot travel upward to the head; there is no pathway in the body that would allow such a movement to occur. But in the Taoist meditation practices, the breathing and mental concentration are used to develop a powerful heat within the abdomen, capable of transforming the *ching* into a vapor. As this vapor becomes very hot, its pressure increases and it is driven through openings at the base of the spine and released upward through the hollow in the center of the spinal column. For those who have actually achieved this through the practice of meditation, the powerful feelings associated with the experience leave no doubt about what is occurring. For those whose understanding of it relies on concepts and theoretical descriptions, there is plenty of room for confusion about just what is supposed to happen and whether or not it is physiologically possible.

On the basis of what has been said so far in this chapter, it should be apparent to the reader that the actual practice of Taoist meditation is a very subtle matter. Since it is entirely an inner process of spiritual and physical development, it is impossible for anyone to tell for sure whether someone who claims to achieve progress in the techniques is really doing it or not. For this reason, it has always been possible for charlatans to go around pretending to be highly expert, but without having any genuine knowledge of meditation at all. Vast numbers of fraudulent meditation masters have appeared throughout Chinese history, seeking to make a fortune by tricking people into believing that they possessed the secret of "immortality." Such charlatanism was always especially prevalent among those who claimed to teach the *shuang hsiu* methods, since the prospect of happiness through sexual fulfillment in addition to immortality was so desirable to many people, and also since it afforded the self-styled master an opportunity to take advantage of gullible people in sexual as well as financial ways. But fraud was also common among teachers of the solitary methods. It was quite easy for people to develop sophisticated ways of talking about the theories involved in real meditation, so that no one would suspect that their own practice consisted of nothing more than sitting half-asleep with their eyes closed. And the material rewards that could be gained by achieving recognition as a meditation master were sometimes quite significant, for many emperors were very interested in discovering the secret of immortality. They were besieged by countless "masters," each offering to reveal the unique true method known only to himself. There are many Chinese folk stories about people who cheat others, even their families or themselves, by appearing to meditate, while really only going through the motions. Some are quite humorous, such as the one about the hen-pecked husband who wished to escape his jealous wife in order to have an affair with a beautiful dancer. The wife treated him almost like a prisoner, keeping track of his whereabouts so closely that there seemed to be no chance for him to develop a relationship with another woman. But after much thought, he figured out a plan of action. He became highly enthusiastic about health and longevity and pretended to become a student under a Taoist meditation master. After a time he explained to his wife that in order to make further progress in meditation, it would be necessary for him to isolate himself from her for a long time in order to practice intensively without interruption. And so he shut himself away in a remote part of their rather large house and spent most of his time sitting in a darkened room meditating. After this had gone on only a short time, however, he instructed a trusty servant to sit in his place, while he sneaked away for a rendezvous with his girlfriend. Soon this became a regular habit, and the servant sat there in the darkened room almost every night. The nosy wife regularly came by to check up on her husband, of course, but when she glanced through the curtain into the darkened room, she could not tell that the meditator was a servant instead of her husband.

After this had gone on for several months, however, she decided to investigate more carefully, and so she quietly entered the room where the meditator was sitting. One can well imagine her surprise and anger when she discovered the servant there in her husband's place. She was about to punish him severely, but he vigorously protested that he knew nothing and was merely following his master's orders. So she spared him, with a stern warning that if he said anything at all to her husband about her discovery, he would surely pay for it with his life. As an extra precaution, she locked the servant in a closet. Then she herself sat down in the servant's place and awaited her husband's return. Sure enough, he came by at dawn, feeling very happy after spending the night with his girlfriend. Thinking the seated meditator was his servant, he began bragging about his affair, talking about what a fine lover his girlfriend was, what a wonderful relationship he had with her, and how they would surely be married if he could ever manage to escape from the awful witch who was his present wife. The wife heard it all without making any reply. But when her husband proceeded to lie down to get some sleep after the night's events, she got up and went over to him and grasped him tightly by the ear. Still mistaking her for his servant, he reacted angrily, exclaiming, "How can you be so disrespectful toward your master?" Giving the ear a twist, she replied, "Judging from what you yourself have just confessed, it's quite clear that you are the one who has been most disrespectful."

NOTES

1. See *Tai Chi Ch'uan and I Ching*, New York: Harper and Row, 1978; *Taoist Health Exercise Book*, New York: Quick Fox, 1974; and "T'ai Chi Ch'uan and Meditation" (forthcoming).

2. See Joseph Needham, *Science and Civilization in China*, Cambridge University Press, 1956, vol. 2, p. 377.

3. *Chuang Tzu*, ch. 11; see *The Texts of Taoism (TT)*, trans. James Legge, Oxford University Press, 1891, vol. 1, p. 298.

4. See *TT*, vol. 1, p. 59.

5. *The Works of Mencius*, part 2, ch. 35; see *The Chinese Classics (CC)*, trans. James Legge, vol. 2, Hong Kong University Press, 1960, p. 497.

6. *Chuang Tzu*, ch. 6; see *TT*, vol. 1, p. 297.

7. *Chuang Tzu*, ch. 3, 1st para. The English translators generally fail to perceive this level of significance in the passage, however. See *TT*, vol. 1, p. 198, for example.

8. *Chuang Tzu*, ch. 15; see *TT*, vol. 1, p. 364.

9. See *CC*, vol. 2, pp. 188–89.

10. See Needham, *op. cit.*, vol. 2, p. 330.

11. Wu Lu-Ch'ian and T.L. Davis, "An Ancient Chinese Treatise on Alchemy Entitled Ts'an T'ung Ch'i," *ISIS*, vol. 18, 1932, p. 210.

12. Thus, for example, the Buddhist sect known as the "Pure Land School," which originated in Tibet, taught a meditation technique which aimed at enabling the consciousness to leave the body just before the moment of death to be reborn in the "pure land." See Lu K'uan Yu (Charles Luk), *The Secrets of Chinese Meditation*, New York: Samuel Weiser, 1972, ch. 3 and p. 198.

13. *TT*, vol. 1, p. 54.

14. Lu K'uan Yu, *Taoist Yoga, Alchemy and Immortality*, New York: Sàmuel Weiser, 1973, ch. 15.

15. *Ibid.*

16. See, for example, A. Ishihara and H.S. Levy, *The Tao of Sex*, Tokyo: Shibundo, 1968, reprinted by Harper and Row: New York, 1970; and also Jolan Chang, *The Tao of Love and Sex: The Ancient Chinese Way to Ecstasy*, New York: E.P. Dutton, 1977.

17. See Needham, *op. cit.*, vol. 2, sec. 10 (i) (4).

chapter 9
TAOiSM ANd MEdiciNE

Aspects of Taoism that increase longevity and retard the aging
process have always appealed to the upper classes of China. Many of
the emperors were wealthy enough to seek out the advice of Taoist
sages in order to pursue these goals. At the same time, however, the
vast majority of Chinese people were faced with much more
fundamental survival problems. Struggling to get enough to eat
precluded their spending any leisure time with Taoist mentors, and
diseases kept the life expectancy among peasants very low. Nevertheless, health practices connected with Taoism were deeply rooted in
the folk traditions of the Chinese countryside, so both rich and poor
applied them to treat and cure diseases. In this sense, Taoism and
medicine reflect all aspects of Chinese culture.

Among the emperors most fascinated with the prospect of
immortality was Ch'in Shih Hwang Ti, who unified the empire in 221
B.C. His military victories brought an end to the Period of the
Warring States and enabled him to unify the country into a single
China for the first time in centuries. Under his absolute rule, rivals
and dissidents were ruthlessly suppressed. Certainly no rich idler who
sought immortality out of boredom, Ch'in Shih Hwang Ti sought
instead to conquer death as aggressively as he had conquered worldly

obstacles. He conducted an imperial tour of Ch'i to consult with Taoist sages and magicians on the prospects of immortality. Tao master Hsü Fu told him of islands off the coast of China where grasses grew that could prevent death and even restore corpses to life. He was also told of the immortal An Ch'i Sheng, a native of these islands, who survived on a diet of dates as large as melons. The mighty warrior emperor was fascinated by these stories and decided he must possess such marvelous plants. He sent a great expedition— according to some accounts, 3,000 young men and 3,000 young women—to find these miraculous islands, but they never returned. They may have reached Japan, but the emperor avidly believed it was sea monsters that prevented their return. He died hunting these monsters near the mouth of the Yellow River. The irony of such a tale would not be lost on followers of Tao.

Farfetched as the legend may seem to us today, it points out the connection between health and nutrition. Throughout the centuries, Taoists have experimented with almost every conceivable substance —mineral, plant, animal—in order to determine its nutritional and medicinal value. A guiding principle for such experimentation has been that nutrition essential to life can be obtained from three sources: heaven, earth, and animals. Heaven is the source of air and the beneficial rays of the sun and moon. Earth contains minerals and plants of great nutritive and medicinal value: mica and quartz crystals, ginseng root, and so on. Such animals as the tortoise and the reindeer have been found to offer healthful by-products. Even the human body is a source of Taoist potions and elixirs. Saliva, blood, and milk are thought to contain essential nutrients not obtainable from other sources; the human placenta is an especially valuable source of nutrients.

Another emperor noted for his interest in longevity methods was Han Wu Ti (140-97 B.C.), whose military conquests in Korea, Mongolia, and Vietnam significantly expanded the territory of the empire. Moreover, his organization of the government established the principles of Confucianism as the orthodox philosophy of the empire for more than two millennia. Some of his immortality practices involved public works projects on a grandiose scale. For example, he ordered the construction of a large earthen mound, on top of which were placed bronze statues of men bearing dew-collecting trays. Each morning, the dew was gathered from these trays and mixed with powdered jade. This tonic was then served to the emperor to increase longevity.

Obviously, the natural substances that compose the human body—flesh, bones, blood, and so on—are not sufficiently durable to last indefinitely. Even with special care, the tissues of the body are likely to deteriorate and die after little more than a century. Perhaps, then, it was concluded by Han Wu Ti and others that one must transform the tissues into more long-lasting substances in order to prolong life. According to such reasoning, the secret of longevity for buildings is that stone and metal survive longer than clay or wood. Thus, Han Wu Ti reasoned, he would transform his tissues by consuming jade mixed with the moisture of the heavens.

Other Taoists experimented with a variety of other mineral substances and metals, developing an esoteric and complex compendium of pseudo-scientific alchemical knowledge. The purpose of such experimentation was to develop a recipe for *tan* (elixir, or golden pill), a substance capable of producing immortality and everlasting youth. Toward this end, Taoists combined the five metals and eight stones in varied proportions and according to sometimes arcane procedures. Of the five metals the most important are mercury and lead. The others are gold, silver, and native copper. The eight stones are cinnabar, mica, realgar, orpiment, sulphur, rock salt, nitre, and k'ung-ch'ing, a green hollow mineral produced in Szu-Chuan Province. Fire was considered essential for purification of the life-giving substance, and some sources refer to it as *lien tan* (fire-purified elixir). In a less philosophical context, fire served to liquefy, sublimate, and boil ingredients so that chemical reactions could take place. As in the case of those experimenting with herbal medicines, these efforts—though based on perhaps unattainable goals—led to chemical discoveries of genuine medical value. In addition, they developed methods of working with metals and other mineral substances that could be applied to technological endeavors outside the field of medicine.

Since ancient times, Chinese physicians have regarded the human body as a microcosm that reflects and obeys the same laws as those which govern the universe as a whole. These laws—including such basic concepts as the alternation of the opposing, complementary forces of Yin and Yang, the relationships among the five elements, and so on—are characterized in such classic writings as the *Nei Ching.* This text organized and united many aspects of traditional thought and Chinese culture within a single conceptual framework, and those who studied such classics were considered qualified to act competently in both philosophical and physiological matters. The reasoning implicit in such a belief belies the exclusive emphasis of the classics in traditional education and accounts for the old folk saying, "The best physician also makes the best statesman."

The concepts of the *Nei Ching* and the five-elements tradition were not invented by Taoists. They must be considered as the heritage of all forms of thought indigenous to China, regardless of their philosophical emphasis. Various schools of thought did, however, influence the development of their application. Confucianists, for example, stressed their application to society and government, while Taoist interpretations of their symbolism were applied to the areas of health and medicine.

A principle premise of the *Nei Ching* is that good health is achieved through a balance between opposing forces, represented most generally by the opposition between Yin and Yang. When either of the forces becomes too dominant, the system is out of balance and illness results. Thus, diseases were classified in opposing pairs: substantial (strong) and insubstantial (weak), hot and cold, internal and external, Yin and Yang. Classifying disorders in this fashion implied consequent methods of treatment, for it was believed that health could be restored by returning the body to a balanced state. If the patient was diagnosed as too strong, the remedy was to reduce strength and energy; if too weak, the remedy was to build up strength. If the problem was classified as too much heat concentrated inside the body, an effort was made to disperse it. The trigrams and hexagrams of the *Nei Ching*, capable of representing complex combinations of Yin and Yang influences, permitted the systems of classification and diagnosis to become quite elaborate.

The five-elements tradition was as important as the *Nei Ching* for the organization of ideas pertaining to health and the treatment of disease. According to this theory, the human body (like all other physical systems) is composed of five fundamental forms of energy or elementary processes: wood, fire, earth, metal, and water. Relationships between these processes are allegedly subject to cyclic laws that govern the flows of energy between them. Because internal organs of the body are identified with the five forms of energy, deductions about the five elements could be applied to the care of the body. The liver and gall bladder were associated with wood, the heart and small intestine with fire, the stomach and spleen with earth, the lungs and large intestine with metal, and the kidneys and bladder with water. Consequently, treatment of disease in these organs was manifested by the physician's knowledge of the five elements.

A major application of such theories emanated from the techniques of acupuncture, a highly sophisticated treatment of ailments with no known paralled in Western medicine. There is a network of pathways on the surface of the body called meridians, which connect the inner organs and constitute channels through which energy can pass. When energy is applied to or withdrawn from a meridian, the inner state of balances between the organs is affected. In acupuncture, needles apply pressure to those points on the meridians that are most effective to desired results: tonification points, sedation points, or source points. The contemporary practitioner of acupuncture has more than a thousand such points at his disposal.

Acupuncture and its derivative forms of treatment cannot easily be assessed in Western terms. Modern Western medical practices rely on techniques that have been tested scientifically before they can be used on the public. However, acupuncture treatments involve invisible processes that often defy measurement by scientific instruments. The flow of energy through the pathways and meridians of the body is an example of such an invisible process. Indeed, these processes appear to resist scientific explanation in part because they are based on psychological and spiritual precepts outside the realm of empirical study. Nevertheless, traditional methods of treatment have frequently cured diseases when more up-to-date scientific methods have failed. Several years of study and practice are required before a practitioner is sufficiently sensitive to manipulate these meridians with needles, massage, and like techniques. One cannot easily ascribe a precise scientific explanation to this acquired sensitivity, yet the benefits of such a skill are irrefutable. I saw Dr. Chia Lin Song cure a student of mine whose arm had been numb for over a year. The student had consulted several Western physicians, but without relief. Shortly after Dr. Song touched his rib, however, his arm recovered completely and the feeling in it was entirely restored. Such evidence is difficult to refute.

During treatment, methods of diagnosis traditionally rely on four methods of observation: the appearance and color of the face, the sound quality of the voice, answers to questions regarding possible symptoms, and the reading of the pulse. Perceptions involved in obtaining this information are subtle and require serious training to detect. For example, the Chinese technique for reading the pulse is more complex than that practiced in the West. Six distinct pulse components relate information about two different inner organs. Moreover, a skilled physician can use these findings to discern psychological conditions and even predict the patient's destiny. Because it is not limited to the empirical strictures of Western medicine, the Chinese physician applies his training to physical, mental, and spiritual prognoses.

Ancient Chinese medical discoveries occurred in semi-legendary times. It is traditionally believed that Shen Nung, the Divine Farmer, initiated the cultivation and experimentation with herbs and grasses in the twenty-ninth century B.C., aspiring to cure the sick. Other early developments are attributed to Hwang Ti, the prototypical Taoist figure who was first to cite methods of detecting specific diseases according to specific symptoms. The oldest Chinese medical treatise, the *Nei Ching*, records a series of discussions between Hwang Ti and his chief medical officer, Ch'i Po. Among the topics covered are the diagnosis and prognosis of diseases and methods of curing them. Other works that record Hwang Ti's theoretical discussions with his officials include the *Lin Shun Ching* and the *Yu Nu Ching*. In the latter, the official is a female, and the discussion mainly concerns sexuality and sexual practices. If these works could be considered accurate records of medical knowledge in Hwang Ti's time, they would warrant the conclusion that techniques of diagnosis and cure were remarkably well-developed in 2600 B.C. Most scholars note, however, that these accounts were not printed until the Han dynasty, by which time the original concepts had been scrutinized and augmented by countless scholars.

Medical practices in China before the Han dynasty remain undocumented. Stories suggest that great physicians did exist in those times—notably, Pien Ch'io and T'sang Kung who lived in the Chou dynasty. The *Lieh Tzu*, a Taoist work of the Warring States period, describes, for example, a successful heart transplant by Pien Ch'io. These accounts are not reliable historical sources, however, and more accurate records have apparently not survived. One reason for this is the famous burning of the books ordered by Ch'in Shih Hwang Ti after his victory in 221 B.C. But it should also be kept in mind that methods of writing were primitive in early times and medical treatises were never widely available.

During the cultural renaissance of the Han dynasty, more reliable resources attested to the development of fairly advanced chemical technology and sophisticated medical techniques. Moreover, recent archeological discoveries in China have provided a firsthand glimpse at both the successes and limitations of medicine at that time. Excavated tombs from the Han dynasty reveal corpses and other perishable objects in remarkably good condition. A 1972 excavation near Ch'angsha in Hunan Province[1] uncovered the entombed body of an aristocratic woman. Some experts say she may have been a consort of the Emperor Han Wu Ti. Others believe she was the wife of the first Marquis of Tai. The corpse was remarkably free of decay; the skin was elastic and fresh and the joints were pliant. According to chemical analysis, the corpse and some other objects in the grave had been treated with a fluid containing organic acids and compounds of mercury. The use of mercury is fascinating, because this element is known to have been widely used by Taoist alchemists who sought to preserve the body indefinitely with the help of chemicals. X-ray examination of the corpse by Chinese scientists showed that the woman, probably a victim of heart attack, also suffered from tuberculosis, gallstones, internal parasites, rheumatism, and lower back pain. Also in the tomb were found small quantities of herbal medicine which medical treatises of the period prescribed for heart disease and which are sometimes used by traditional physicians even to this day.

Other Han period tomb excavations have uncovered bodies encased in jade which have also remained amazingly well-preserved. These discoveries throw light on the efforts of early Han physicians. Apparently, they put greatest emphasis on chemical methods by which youthful freshness could be preserved. In treating functional disorders, however, their methods were somewhat less advanced, suggesting more interest in finding the secret to everlasting life than in healing immediate ailments. As of the second century B.C., they had at least discovered the secret of lasting preservation after death. This irony aside, their success is evidence of a chemical technology far more advanced than what would be known elsewhere in the world for many centuries to come.

It is likely that the active interest in the secrets of immortality exhibited by Han Wu Ti and members of the ruling aristocracy created favorable conditions for invention and new ideas. For example, the *Hwei Nan Tzu* was written by Liu An—prince of Hwei Nan and uncle of Han Wu Ti—who was deeply interested in immortality. But Liu An was also so interested in chemical and alchemical developments that he directed research efforts that may have involved hundreds of people. Among the results of these efforts, a process was invented to make soy beans into bean curd. This chemical discovery contributed to the realization of Taoist principles, for it provided nutritious protein without the need to kill animals. Today, this high-protein food is popular all over the world, and Western vegetarians are especially fond of it.

The state of medical practice in the early Han dynasty is known mainly as a result of the interests of the emperors and aristocrats. Later in the dynasty's reign, however, a number of physicians achieved independent fame, and their own writings detail their methods. Some of these physicians, who were also Taoists, apparently regarded the study of medicine as an aspect of Taoist practice. Perhaps the most famous of these was Chang Chi (also known as Chang Chung Ching). He rose to a high official position as governor of Ch'angsha, but after many members of his clan died of pneumonia, he resigned his post to devote full time to writing and the study of medicine. Among his treatises, perhaps the greatest is the *Shang Han Lun* (Knowledge about Pneumonia and Influenza), which has been consulted by Chinese physicians even in recent times. After his death, Chang Chung Ching came to be honored as the "Second Sage of Medicine" because of his many contributions and achievements in that field.

Another late Han dynasty figure noted both as physician and Taoist was Hwa T'o, also known as Hwa Yuan Hwa. A typical Taoist, he refused opportunities to become a government official, even though his knowledge and scholarship greatly impressed the emperor. Hwa devoted his time to the study of all aspects of medicine, including the use of drugs, acupuncture, and even surgery. He is said to have performed abdominal and back operations in order to repair inner organs and cure diseases. His fame grew after he saved the life of the great General Kwan Yu (also known as Kwan Kung) who had been wounded by a poison arrow. However, Hwa plotted to assassinate the powerful Ts'ao Ts'ao, who later became king of Wei during the Three Kingdoms period. The plot failed and Hwa was imprisoned. Like many Taoists before him, Hwa T'o's involvement in political rebellion eventually cost him his life.

Formerly, Hwa had kept his methods secret and had not taught students. But before his death in prison, he made an effort to preserve his medical knowledge for posterity. He approached a prison official who appeared to be sympathetic and gave him some writings— entitled simply *Ch'ing Non* (Green Package)—in which instructive techniques were described. Hwa hoped that the official would study them and make them available, to the benefit of others. Unfortunately, the official's wife burned the manuscript, and Hwa T'o's vast knowledge died with him. This was a great loss, for future historians have had to rely on legends reconstructing his apparently advanced procedures. Among the techniques he developed, however, a few are still known today. Among them, the "Five Animals Health Exercises" imitate the natural behavior of five kinds of animals. These are explained in detail in one of my earlier books.[2]

During the centuries of disorder following the end of the Han dynasty, the techniques of medicine continued to develop. The study of herbs and chemicals became more systematic and the medical value of substances was classified and catalogued. A great contributor toward this effort was T'ao Hung Ching (451-536), a noted Taoist physician, alchemist, botanist, and prolific writer. This native of the region south of the Yangtze River, now in Chiang-su Province, became well-known for his scholarship in early life and was appointed as an official under the northern Ch'i emperor. In typical Taoist fashion, T'ao resigned his post, retreated to the Chu Yung Mountains, and lived as a recluse in Hwa Yang cave. His interests encompassed all aspects of Taoist life: meditation, cosmology and divination, herbal medicine, and alchemy. When the Buddhist Emperor Liang Wu Ti in the south heard of his reputation, he was eager to appoint him as an adviser. The emperor promised to supply him with such rare materials as gold and mercury for his alchemical research. But in reply, the Taoist painted a picture and sent it to Liang Wu Ti. The picture represented two oxen, one of which was free to roam about, eating grass and drinking as he pleased, while the other was confined by a golden halter and driven by a man with a whip. The Emperor Liang Wu Ti smiled when he saw the painting, for he realized that he could not lure T'ao Ching from his mountain retreat. Nonetheless, he often sent messengers to consult the Taoist sage about affairs of state. In fact, T'ao Hung Ching became known as the Premier in the Mountains; and he was also called the Perfect Man of Hwa Yang, after the name of his cave dwelling.

Of T'ao Hung Ching's many writings, perhaps the most important from a medical point of view was his *Pen Ts'ao* (Materia Medica). Thousands of varieties of plants—including trees, grasses, fungi, flowers, and fruits—are there identified and classified according to their medical uses. His was not the first manual of this kind, but *Pen Ts'ao* is more complete than its predecessors. Also unusual is its emphasis on herbs to the exclusion of other substances—such as stone, metals, fish, insects, and other animal products. According to an old legend, T'ao Hung Ching long had practiced techniques of meditation and alchemy but was puzzled that he had still not become immortal. Eventually, when one of his students, Huan K'ai, successfully achieved immortality, T'ao Hung Ching said to him, "I have been practicing all the methods diligently for much longer than you have, yet you have attained the goal before me. Please ask the superior gods why I progress so slowly toward immortality." According to the story, Huan K'ai consulted the gods and returned to report to his master: "You have been writing too many medical treatises, in which the use of creatures for medicine is described. Such knowledge may be useful for mankind, enabling one to cure diseases, but it will surely cause other animals to be harmed and destroyed in the process." Upon hearing this report, T'ao Hung Ching went back to his writings and reworked them, removing all references to the killing of animals and emphasizing instead the use of herbs. During the T'ang dynasty, his book was expanded and revised by physicians and scholars, so that it eventually filled seven volumes. Among his other treatises, two are especially worth mentioning because of their medical interest: the *Teng Chen Yin Chueh* (Instructions for Ascending to the True Concealed Ones) and *Yang Seng Yen Ming Lu* (Delaying Destiny by Nourishing Life). The former describes methods of heliotherapy; the latter is included in the *Tao Tsang*, the official canon of Taoist writings, and contains information on sex physiology and practices.

Another famous Taoist physician and herbalist was Sun Ssu Mo (581–682).[3] An account of his life in the *Record of Buddhist and Taoist Immortals*[4] says he was a native of Hwa Yuan in Northwest China and lived for more than a century. A dedicated scholar, Sun grew up studying the writings of Lao Tzu and Chuang Tzu and like classics of Taoist philosophy, plus techniques of medicine, meditation, and divination. By age seven, he reportedly could read a thousand sentences a day. Sun was famous for his dedication to the common people, and his writings describe prescriptions and treatments formerly reserved for the emperor and his officials. After a long medical practice, he retired to become a hermit on T'ai Po San (Great White Mountain). Sun declined all offers of high position for himself, including the honorary title bestowed on him when he was nearly a hundred years old by Emperor T'ang Tai Tsung. Sun's most important medical writing was the *Ch'ien Chin Fong* (Thousand Ounces of Gold Prescriptions), but he wrote many other books as well, including *Discussions of Riches and Health, Nourishing Life*, and *The Prescription Hidden in the Pillow*. Perhaps his greatest contribution was the discovery of an effective cure for smallpox, which saved the lives of millions of children and remained the best treatment for the disease for better than a thousand years. Later generations of Chinese physicians venerated him as "God of Medicine." Even today, his memory is honored by Chinese, regardless of their political persuasions: Both Communist and Nationalist governments have issued postage stamps commemorating his achievements.

Every century has produced great Taoist physicians. Even today, their traditional practices and techniques rival methods of treatment introduced from the West. The Taoist practice of taking herbs and minerals for health and longevity has remained widespread in recent times. In fact, well-documented cases attest to the efficacy of such practices, when they are pursued diligently. Perhaps the most spectacular example is that of Li Ch'ing Yuen, an herbalist by profession, who was allegedly born in 1678 and died at the age of two hundred fifty-five. Journalists discovered his whereabouts in Szechwan Province in the late 1920's and carefully studied his claims. They found that he had been married fourteen times and that the imperial government had officially congratulated him on his 150th and 200th birthdays. Media from all over the world reported his story and, in 1933, even the *New York Times* listed his obituary.

People still alive today, both on Taiwan and on the mainland, were personally acquainted with Li Ch'ing Yuen. These include Li Huan, now a member of the Chinese Nationalist General Assembly on Taiwan, who was mayor of Wanhsien, Szechwan, when Li Ch'ing Yuen lived near there. Li Huan cared for the old man and assisted General Yang Shen in writing a book about the sage's teachings. Another book on Li Ch'ing Yuen, based on first-hand knowledge, was published in Shanghai by Yang Ho Hsuan Chu Jen, another of his students. In the West, two of my own books—*Taoist Health Exercise Book* and *The Tao Of Health And Longevity*—describe some of his health practices in detail. Richard Lucas's book *Nature's Medicines*[5] is also worthy of mention—especially Chapter 14—with regard to Li Ch'ing Yuen.

These sources attribute the great longevity of Li Ch'ing Yuen to several factors. As a professional herbalist, he was aware of plants that can promote health and longevity. He is known to have taken regularly herbs such as ginseng (panax schinseng) and Fo Ti Tieng (Hydrocotyle asiatica minor). But in addition, he practiced many other Taoist techniques—including health exercises and meditation —and lived a peaceful worry-free life in typical Taoist style. He had studied Lao Tzu, Chuang Tzu, and other Taoist classics carefully, and those who knew him reported that he often quoted them when he taught.

Perhaps his story most clearly shows that the scientific laboratory cannot adequately measure the effectiveness of Taoist herbs and chemicals as tools of longevity. True adepts of these techniques did not merely swallow chemical potions; they lived according to practices of which these herbal methods were but a part. No less important was the renunciation of organized society, avoidance of public attention, and advocacy of the eremitic life-style. This understood, it is remarkable that Li Ch'ing Yuen was actually "discovered" by the modern world. It also suggests that the most successful practitioners of the Taoist longevity methods will always be unknown to the world. The wise and lucky ones remain vague, shadowy characters skirting the fringes of society who eventually disappear into the wilderness, never to be seen again. Is it possible that some have been living there in quiet solitude for centuries?

More likely, Li Ch'ing Yien must have been extremely rare. The vast majority of Taoist adepts who consumed immortality potions no doubt failed. Some actually harmed or even fatally poisoned themselves, either because their elixirs were not properly purified or because they had insufficiently prepared themselves as Taoists. Unless they had rid themselves of ignorance, impatience, and carelessness, the powerful elixir could be misdirected with damaging results. Such an account is found in the eighteenth-century novel *The Dream of the Red Chamber*. Widely accepted by scholars as an accurate account of Chinese life in the early Manchu (Ch'ing) dynasty, it chronicles the family of its author, Ts'ao Hsueh-ch'in, the direct descendant of an imperial official. One episode relates the fate of a great uncle of Chia Pao Yu, the autobiographical protagonist. Though an old man, Chia Ging was slated to inherit a military rank of great honor (military general and noble lord, acting as progenitor of the Ning Kuo-Fu, the eastern branch of the Chia family). An ardent Taoist, he passed it on to his son and retired to practice magic, worship the stars and planets, and study with Taoist priests at the monastery Yuen Chen Kwan. In Chapter 63, Chia Ging elected to take a powerful elixir, after which his stomach hardened like stone, his face reddened with sores, and his lips cracked and bled. At first, the family sought to punish the Taoist priests for having poisoned their esteemed uncle, but the priests protested that Chia Ging had taken the elixir despite their warnings. It was, they said, purified by a secret recipe but that they had not considered the old man sufficiently prepared in Taoist teachings to attempt so dynamic a potion. Chia Ging had impatiently ignored their warnings, justifying his eagerness to become immortal with the help of astrological charts. Perhaps he had been correct after all, the Taoists suggested, for his spirit had now indeed become immortal.

This story illustrates a perhaps common outcome that befell rich and powerful pursuers of immortality who lacked the patience and devotion prescribed by Taoist techniques. They sought to get quick results by taking pills, but only harmed themselves when their bodies could not handle the powerful chemicals the medicine contained. According to authentic Taoist teachings, the proper preparation for taking such an elixir must be spiritual as well as physical. As Chuang Tzu says, "Can the body be made to become thus like dry wood and the mind to become like dead ashes."[6] If one has actually achieved such a state of mental emptiness through the constant practice of meditation and other techniques, an elixir can be beneficial without destroying the essential processes of the body. But if the mind is stirred up, anxious to become immortal, scheming for short-cuts to accomplish its aim, the elixir can throw all the inner processes out of proportion and become a means not to everlasting life but to a quick death.

NOTES

1. *National Geographic*, vol. 145, no. 5, May 1974, pp. 660–81.

2. *Taoist Health Exercise Book*, New York: Quick Fox, 1974, pp. 71–72.

3. I have already cited his achievements in one of my earlier books: *The Tao of Health and Longevity*, New York: Schocken Books, 1978, p. 170.

4. *Record of Buddhist and Taoist Immortals*, vol. 1, pp. 99-192, n.d.
5. West Nyack, N.Y., 1966.
6. *The Writings of Chuang Tzu*, in *The Texts of Taoism*, trans. James Legge, Oxford University Press, 1891, p. 176.

CHAPTER 10
hsienship: the highest goal of taoist practice

As we have seen, the Taoist tradition has affected all major aspects of Chinese culture, both in thought (philosophy, political theory, religion) and practice. Meditation, the cultivation and use of herbs, alchemical experimentation, the study of magic, each is imbued with Taoist techniques which reveal important facets of traditional Chinese art and society. Diverse as these techniques may seem, all are closely related by a Taoist goal: the ultimate attainment of physical and spiritual immortality known as "hsien." In "hsienship," we add the English suffix to this Chinese word, but the concept must not be thus too quickly categorized and oversimplified. The Westerner associates immortality with the avoidance of death, but subtle connotations of hsienship elude this interpretation.

The Chinese character for hsien (仙) combines two different symbols. The one on the left depicts a man; that on the right a mountain. Its original meaning is perhaps best rendered as "mountain man," reflecting the traditional view that the immortals live in remote mountain wildernesses, far from the cities. This meaning also refers to a Taoist as "Shan-Jen," a usage frequently preferred by Taoists themselves. Literally, Shan-Jen means "mountain person." Since this closely resembles what is depicted by the "hsien" character, both share connotations of immortality.

The idea of hsienship is to be found in the earliest of Chinese writings. Among the Chinese classics, the *Chuang Tzu* describes it most clearly. Historical records through the centuries cite individuals who have attained hsienship and have made use of the fabulous powers it connotes. Legends found in the *Pa Hsien*, written in the Sung dynasty,* typify the best examples of sincere and vivid belief of Taoists down through the ages. Serious practitioners of Taoism have considered the goal of hsienship really possible, though extremely hard to attain.

Nonetheless, belief in the attainment of immortality is difficult for Westerners and Chinese alike to take seriously. To skeptics, the idea of hsienship represents one more legendary fiction. After all, no one has emerged with a public claim of being an immortal. Indeed, there are no reliable accounts of anyone's even having seen a hsien. If the immortal hsien really exist, one might ask, where are they? What has become of them? To raise such doubts involves dismissing written records spanning countless centuries. It is ludicrous to pretend that all such accounts constitute a hoax, for they represent beliefs deeply ingrained in Chinese culture. In both ancient and modern times, those who attempted to achieve hsienship have encompassed all levels of society: emperors, premiers, scholars, and peasants alike.

A measure of the strength of such beliefs is that accounts of the attainment of hsienship are found not only in the writings of Taoists themselves, but even in the writings of those who strongly oppose Taoism. A good example of this is a long poem written by Han Yü (762–827), the tough-minded Confucianist of the T'ang period who stoutly opposed both Taoism and Buddhism.[1] A naive young girl named Hsieh Tze Jan lived in the district of Nan Ch'ung Hsien in Szechwan Province. She was of humble origins and lacked formal education, yet she became interested in the techniques for achieving immortality and eventually attained such an advanced state of practice that she actually achieved hsienship. The poem describes how she ascended into heaven from the roof of her house, noting that many people witnessed the incident and reported it to the govern-

---

*Most of the Eight Immortals first appeared in the T'ang dynasty; but they were written about in the Sung dynasty.

ment. For our puposes, it is curious to note the poet's tone in this description. For Han Yü, normal activities for a man included plowing; for a woman, weaving; and for all members of the community, support of parents, family, and government. To abandon such goals in pursuit of hsienship was, for him, a moral failing. Han Yü never doubted for a moment that Hsieh Tze Jan did in fact achieve hsienship and rise to heaven; but the blasphemy of her feat infuriated him.

Actually, the concept of hsienship follows naturally from some of the most fundamental ideas of Chinese philosophy, ideas that have shaped Chinese thought since earliest times. Most basic is the assumption that man is a natural component of the universe, comparable to heaven and earth and subject to the same laws of cyclic change. A man who lives in complete harmony with these natural processes can expect to continue existing as long as heaven and earth do, for all are equally affected by their participation in the processes. From this point of view, the unfortunate phenomenon of early death, experienced by the vast majority, is deemed unnatural, the result of destructive human tendencies which interfere with the natural harmony of man and nature. Some mortal weaknesses are physical, having to do with habits of hygiene, diet, and the like; others are psychological and emotional. Accordingly, techniques which aim at hsienship are designed to overcome this destruction and to rejuvenate those who practice them. Various physical and mental disciplines strengthen the body and bring peace to the spirit.

The claim that cyclic changes pertain equally to the natural processes of heaven and earth and to human experience is predicated on the *I Ching*, the most ancient of classic Chinese writings. In fact, the sixty-four hexagrams constitute a detailed representation of all stages of these constantly renewing cycles. A complete account of how this representation works would require far more space than is available here, but it is possible to illustrate the principles involved and to show their pertinence to the concept of hsienship by focusing on just four hexagrams: Ch'ien, K'un, Po, and Fu.

Ch'ien (☰), consisting of entirely unbroken (Yang) lines, represents light, activity, strength, and spirit. Its time of day is noon, its season is summer; or it can signify that time in a person's life when he enjoys the vigor of full maturity. K'un (☷) , consisting of entirely broken (Yin) lines, complements Ch'ien. K'un represents darkness, quiescence, weakness, and yielding. Its hour is midnight, its season is winter, or it can signify the decrepitude of advanced old age. In Po (☶) , all the lines are broken except for the Yang line at the top. Po represents decay and disintegration, a process in which the dark forces gradually overcome the light and the strong. It can describe the dusk, late autumn, and the declining vigor of advancing age. Its complement is Fu (☳) , with a single Yang line at the bottom. Fu represents reverse, return, the turning point at which the light begins to appear in the midst of darkness. It signifies the first glimmer of dawn, the first signs in late winter that spring is approaching, or the time of infancy.

Taken together, these four symbols describe a cycle that repeats itself again and again. Fu represents the beginning of a growth that reaches its acme in Ch'ien, then declines through Po to a point of utter barrenness, or K'un, which is followed once again by Fu, and so on. The cycle continues indefinitely. Thus, the process does not "die" at the low point of K'un. It may appear that the light has completely vanished at midnight or that all plant life has withered and died in mid-winter; in reality this is not the end but only a stage in the cycle, a time of hibernation and rest, soon to be followed once again by revival and renewal.

This interpretation of the course of nature has been accepted by the Chinese as universally true. In such a context, it is entirely plausible to apply the same idea to human life as well. It may appear that all the human vigor of life retreats with the advance of old age, but this does not necessarily mean that death is inevitable. Perhaps it is one's own mid-winter, just another phase of the life cycle which promises continuation into rejuvenation and a return to infancy. The Taoist concept of hsienship is fundamentally based on just such an expectation, and the Taoist techniques developed to attain this goal seek to effect the proper harmony between man and nature in order to expedite this renewal.

The text of the *I Ching* comments on the possibility of attaining such harmony. A particularly good example is found in the commentary of the fifth line of the Ch'ien hexagram:

The great man is he who is in harmony: in his attributes, with heaven and earth; in his brightness, with the sun and the moon; in his orderly procedure, with the four seasons;... He may precede heaven, and heaven will not act in opposition to him; he may follow heaven, but will act only as heaven would at that time.[2]

The ancient Taoist classics are even more explicit in developing the same theme. The fortieth chapter of the *Tao Te Ching*, for example, states:

> Cyclic is the motion of Tao,
> Weakness is the appliance of Tao.[3]

This terse saying affirms the universal principle of cyclical change. Further, its expression concerning the harmony attained with Tao serves as a concrete application of Taoist hsienship techniques: unity with the cycles of nature and avoidance of aggressive action. Extravagant expenditure of energy and great effort to achieve strength and power are excesses which may lead to short-term success, but the ultimate result is an early death. This is clearly stated in Chapter 30 of the *Tao Te Ching*:

> When things come to the pinnacle of their strength, they begin to grow old. This is contrary to Tao, and what is contrary to Tao will soon come to an end.[4]

To achieve unity with Tao, it is essential to pursue an opposite course: to become pliant and yielding, to abide in inaction and conserve energy, to be humble and peaceful in one's approach to life. Society may view the serious cultivation of such habits as failure, but the real reward transcends conventional mores. Harmony with the cycles of nature will allow the natural process of rejuvenation to occur and, perhaps, ultimately lead to immortality. As is written in the tenth chapter of the *Tao Te Ching*: "When one gives undivided attention to vital energy and brings it to an utmost degree of pliancy, one can become like a newborn infant.[5] Passages in the *Writings of Chuang Tzu* elaborate the concepts underlying the pursuit of hsienship. Further, some describe what it is like actually to reach the ultimate goal and become a hsien. For example, the following excerpt is taken from Chapter 1:

> Far away on Ku-she Mountain there lives a hsien whose flesh and skin are [bright and pure] as ice and snow, and who is naturally graceful as a young maiden. He does not eat any of the five grains, but deeply inhales the wind and drinks the dew. Riding the clouds mounted high on a flying dragon, he travels beyond the four seas. By concentrating his spiritual powers he can save men from sickness and pestilence, and can ensure a plentiful harvest each year. . . . Nothing can harm him; a drought so severe that it caused rocks and metals to melt and scorched the earth and hills could not burn him.[6]

This description offers a vivid picture of extraordinary powers that are associated with the attainment of hsienship. It also mentions disciplines commonly practiced by those who aspire to hsienship—dietary restrictions and breathing exercises. The quoted passage does not explicitly mention the extreme longevity attained by the hsien, but Chuang Tzu stresses this aspect of hsienship elsewhere. For example, in his account of the Yellow Emperor's visit to the hsien named Kuang Ch'eng Tzu on K'ung-tung Mountain, the hsien makes the following remark to Hwang Ti:

> Watch over and keep your body, and all things will of themselves give it vigor. I maintain the unity [of Tao] and live in harmony with it. In this way, I have cultivated myself for twelve hundred years, and my body has never gone into decline.[7]

Both the story of Hwang Ti's trip, cited previously in our introduction, to K'ung-tung Mountain and the more recent passage about the hsien on Ku-she Mountain typify early accounts of Taoist immortals.

Note in particular that these legendary figures live in remote, nearly inaccessible mountain areas of Western China. In fact, some of the earliest travel records in these forbidding territories include the journeys of emperors to the immortals who lived there. The earliest such account—Hwang Ti's visit to Kuang Ch'eng Tzu—is not only recounted in Chuang Tzu's writings, but also in such historical records as the biography of Hwang Ti by the first-century historian Ssuma Ch'ien. Ssuma Ch'ien actually retraced the Yellow Emperor's steps to K'ung-tung Mountain and based his account partly on the oral accounts of natives in that area. Another such journey was undertaken by Emperor Mu of the Chou dynasty, who reigned from 1023 to 983 B.C. According to the *Annals of the Bamboo Books*, the journey began in Loyang, whence the emperor crossed the Yellow River, traveled through what is now Shansi Province and Inner Mongolia, passed the high K'un Lun Mountain range, and finally arrived at the shore of the Ch'ing Hai.* There he met Hsih Wong Mo (Western Queen Mother), a female hsien who was later worshipped as an important goddess of the Taoist religion.

These ancient accounts generally describe the immortal hsien as dwelling in the western mountains, suggesting to the historian perhaps that the cult of hsienship probably originated in that part of China. More likely, however, it merely reflects the generally Western orientation of civilization during the early Chou period. After the Chou emperors moved their capital to Loyang, the focus of civilization changed also, moving eastward. Consequently, the cultural and historical traditions of the people living near the seacoast became more widely known and emphasized.

By that time, Taoist concepts—including that of hsienship—had already been influential for centuries in such states as Ch'i and Yen. According to the legends originating in these area, immortal hsien lived on islands off the coast. These legends had a particularly strong effect on Ch'in Shih Hwang Ti, the king of the westerly Ch'in state who, as conqueror of the state of Ch'i, brought an end to the Warring States period and became emperor. After he became aware of these stories while touring the areas near the sea, he grew obsessed with discovering these islands and obtaining the magic herbs said to grow there. By the time of Emperor Han Wu Ti (140–97 B.C.), the eastern and western traditions were accepted equally, and it became commonplace to distinguish between the hsien of the mountains and the hsien of the sea.

In Chinese literature throughout the centuries, countless terms have been used to refer to the immortal hsien. They have been called "sages," "real" or "true men of old," "gods," "witches," "men with

---

*The Green Sea, also called Western Sea, but actually a large lake in what is now Chinghai Province.

magic powers," and sometimes simply "alchemists." But by the time of the Sung dynasty, the pursuit of hsienship became a highly regimented practice of Taoist religion. A unified terminology evolved, and the hsien were even classified according to an ascending scale of ranks befitting their level of accomplishment. For those who strove to learn and practice the sundry Taoist techniques—particularly within institutionalized forms of Taoism that developed during the T'ang and Sung periods—these ranks perhaps resembled such academic levels of achievement as B.A., M.A., Ph.D., and the various professorial ranks. The analogy breaks down, however, since the rewards associated with the achievement of hsienship are incomparably more worthwhile.

At the lowest level is the Kuei Hsien (Ghost Immortal), who achieves spiritual but not physical immortality. Though he cannot avoid death, his continual practice of meditation and other Taoist techniques over a long period of time enables him to concentrate his spirit and maintain presence in the world even after his body has died and decayed. It is thought that Lao Tzu refers to this level of hsienship when he says, "He who dies and yet does not perish, has longevity."[8]

An analogy may clarify the kind of immortality enjoyed by the Kuei Hsien. I recently read a newspaper account of a theater near Times Square in New York City which is believed to be haunted by a ghost. During performances of plays in this theater, a strange voice can be heard at times in the background, either laughing or weeping, depending on whether the play being performed is a comedy or a tragedy. Some have also reported bizarre apparitions but said that they disappeared when anyone tried to approach them. A veteran actor, when he heard of these reports, suggested they were the ghost of one David Belasco, an actor who had performed in the theater for many years on a regular basis and had achieved fame and success there. So great was the concentration of his energy that even after his death the power of a lifetime remained in that building as a spiritual presence. Although the Kuei Hsien are not limited to any single location, this is substantially the same idea as that involved in the lowest level of hsienship.

At the second level of hsienship is the Jen Hsien (Human

Immortal). His practice of meditation and other techniques is so highly advanced that he avoids death by achieving rejuvenation of the body (Fu), becoming once again like a newborn babe. Such people experience outstanding good health, never suffering from sickness or pain, and can live for centuries. Yet they are still human beings, and in many respects have quite human limitations. A man who apparently achieved this level of hsienship was Li Ch'ing Yuen, the remarkable sage who died at the age of 250, soon after his story became known throughout the world. His eventual death is discussed later in this chapter.

The next highest level, the Ti Hsien (Earthly Immortal), achieves not only rejuvenation but a variety of extraordinary powers that go far beyond the accomplishments of ordinary humans. He can survive indefinitely without eating everyday foods, can walk hundreds of miles a day, is unaffected by extreme weather conditions, can be neither drowned nor burned. As Lao Tzu says, "Poisonous insects will not sting him; fierce beasts will not seize him; birds of prey will not strike him."[9] In addition, he possesses some magical powers. A famous example of a hsien of this rank is the Sung dynasty Taoist Chang San Feng, widely recognized as inventor of the system of martial arts and health exercise known as T'ai Chi Ch'uan.

At the next ascending level is the T'ien Hsien (Heavenly Immortal). He has all the powers of the Ti Hsien and is also able to fly into the heavens and ride among the clouds, propelled at great speed by the winds. He can also attain extreme longevity and has much more powerful magic at his disposal, including the ability to control the weather. The hsien of Ku-she′ Mountain described in the passage from Chuang Tzu quoted above was obviously a T'ien Hsien. So was Lu Tung Pin, the great T'ang dynasty immortal described in Chapter 7 above.

Finally, at the highest level is the Ta Lo Chin Hsien (Golden Immortal). Unlimited by conditions of space and time, he can appear in the form of a man or in any other shape at any location in heaven or on earth during any moment of the past, present, or future, solely according to his power of mental concentration; and he can just as easily disappear. He lives in the heavens or in human society, depending on what is most suitable to his current purposes, but even if heaven and earth were destroyed, he would continue to exist. Individuals who have actually attained so godlike an existence are not easily documented, for legends surrounding this ultimate form of hsienship remain fairly vague as to details. However, some Taoists hold that belief in the existence of this highest level is based on Chapter 25 of the *Tao Te Ching*, whose fourth paragraph mentions all the ranks of hsienship except the lowest:

> Man takes his law from Earth;
> The Earth takes its law from Heaven;
> Heaven takes its law from the Tao;
> The law of the Tao simply is.[10]

The very highest goal of hsienship, then, means actually reaching complete unity with Tao. Our preliminary discussion in the Introduction noted how difficult it is to define Tao; understandably, then, it is no easier fully to describe the personal identity of someone who has actually reached such an affinity.

More recent Chinese literature and spoken tradition show an interesting difference in points of view toward those who devote their lives to the advanced practice of Taoist techniques in the pursuit of immortality. Some picture them as good men, rather mysterious but very gentle and benevolent toward others. Just as frequently, however, one hears them portrayed as drunken, dissolute bums whose extremes of laziness and filth make them fitting objects of scorn, if not pity. What these differing perceptions really show, I think, is that there is far more to the achievement of hsienship than meets the eye. Whether someone has actually attained it becomes a subtle issue. A fine line separates those whose renunciation of ordinary society and serious practice of Taoism has resulted in success and those whose similar course has resulted in madness. Similarly, no clear, unambiguous criteria determine a person's true situation on the basis of his behavior. An old man covered with grime may be seen sitting all day without speaking or perhaps may be heard babbling nonsense in response to a question. Such a person may be a real hsien, who pretends to be a madman in order to protect himself from the great notoriety that would result were his possession of extraordinary powers to become known to the public. Indeed, according to traditional accounts, rags are a standard disguise by which hsien cloak their identities. Even the great Chang San Feng— inventor of T'ai Ch'i Chuan—came to be known by the nickname "Dirty Chang." On the other hand, the jabbering reprobate may be only a bum or a madman of negligible spiritual depth who pretends to be a hsien by affecting strange behavior. He may even be crafty enough to encourage his fraud further by the help of such props as swords, herbs, or other trappings of Taoist practice. The ultimate truth or falsity of the achievement of hsienship is internal, so the outward appearance of the hsien is inevitably ambiguous.

As a young man, I studied for a time in Chenkiang, capital of Kiangsu Province. The Chin Shan Szu (Golden Mountain Temple), located beside the Yangtze River, was a famous center of Buddhist activity. Many masters of meditation could be found there, as well as people at all levels of practice striving for immortality. According to what I was told by local people, a monk in the area was a real hsien, hundreds of years old. He could not be seen at the temple, however. In fact, there was no definite place where one could expect to meet him. Yet as I went about the city and the surrounding countryside, I would occasionally see a very old man sitting quietly alone. He never seemed to be in the same place twice. Sometimes, he was on the path at the foot of a hill; other times, he would be at the roadside or even in a marketplace or other public spot. He never spoke to anyone and ignored those who tried to strike up a conversation with him. When harassed by a persistent questioner, he would open his mouth and loudly chant "Amitofu," a name of the Buddha. Some people said that he had been there as long as they could remember and had never changed in appearance. Some even said that their own grandfathers had told them the same thing. But who really was this old man, and what was he actually doing? No one could be certain of anything beyond the fact that he was an ambiguous image in traditional Chinese culture.

This same ambiguity is the basis of many amusing anecdotes. Such is the story of a man who regularly left his wife and went off into the mountains for long periods to fast and practice Taoist methods. His wife was very patient with this, for she knew that before too long he would grow disillusioned with the rigors of such a life and would return home for food and other supplies. On one occasion, he was gone for a particularly long time, but when he finally ran out of supplies entirely, he came down from the mountains tired and very hungry. When he arrived home, he saw from a distance that his wife was busy baking pies. She had set some out to cool and was now rolling out the dough in order to make a second batch. She was so preoccupied with her work that she did not notice he was approaching. Before he even greeted her, the ravenous pilgrim stepped lightly and carefully to the window sill so as not to be detected and, without a word as yet to his wife, snatched one of the cooling pastries. As he greedily devoured it, an exciting thought occurred to him: "Perhaps I really have achieved hsienship at last, and she cannot see me because I've become invisible!" He decided to test his theory (and his appetite) by sneaking a second pie. But this time, his wife grabbed her rolling pin and whacked him sharply across the buttocks. He jumped with surprise and exclaimed, "Why are you beating me? After I ate the first pie, I thought I had become a hsien, since you weren't able to see me!" His wife laughed and replied, "I thought you'd gone crazy, so I decided to ignore you!"

As this story illustrates, the achievement of hsienship is an ambiguous matter. In fact, the illusion of immortality was not rare in Chinese traditional society. In many instances, people have genuinely made claims to the public that they had indeed achieved immortality, only to suffer embarrassment and other unfortunate consequences when their health subsequently declined. Such a fate befell Wang Hsien Ch'ing, formerly a Kuomintang official in Shanghai, who stayed at his post after the Japanese invasion. Several years later, I used to meet him often in a park in Taipei, where I practiced T'ai Chi Ch'uan early in the morning. We enjoyed many an interesting discussion about Taoist philosophy and practices, from which I deduced that he was extremely knowledgeable and highly advanced in these matters. I was not alone in being impressed with him, and as his reputation grew, he became a popular lecturer, for which he was advertised and introduced as an actual hsien. Apparently, he himself believed that he was immortal, for he never denied these claims. He also thought it unnecessary to eat grain or other ordinary foods, with the result that his body suffered from lack of nourishment. Some years later, while in New York, I came across a magazine report of his demise. One of his legs had become paralyzed and eventually had to be amputated. Weakened beyond help due to his long improper eating habits, he failed to recover successfully, and his immortality was laid to rest with his remains, exposed as an illusion.

Even those who may truly be considered as hsien are liable to lose their powers and suffer death. This can come about if their lives change in ways that interfere with or interrupt their extraordinary devotion to meditation and other practices. The realization of the rejuvenation process which prevents death and decay is a great achievement indeed; but to sustain this process indefinitely proves an even greater task. Countless aspirants to hsienship have lost everything and perished after becoming momentarily distracted by women, money, or fame. Perhaps even the death of the remarkable Li Ch'ing Yuen can be regarded as an example of this, for his life ended not long after he interrupted his regular habits of conduct in order to move from K'ai-hsien to Wanhsien city at the invitation of General Yang Sen. In Wanhsien, he was kept rather preoccupied discussing his longevity practices with crowds of eager students and was the focus of considerable attention. Not long after he returned to his home, Li Huan, Yang Sen's envoy in Nanking, told Chiang K'ai-shek about him and showed him his picture. Chiang expressed considerable interest in meeting with Li Ch'ing Yuen, but when they telegraphed to arrange a liaison, they learned that Li Ch'ing Yuen had died shortly after his return home from Wanhsien. No one could identify the precise cause of death. Perhaps he had become ill as a result of a change in his diet. Perhaps he had worn himself out by talking too much. Perhaps he simply did not wish to experience the consequences of such widespread fame. In any case, his story illustrates how distraction could interrupt the career of a Taoist immortal, even one whose achievement of hsienship was apparently quite genuine.

A more clear-cut example concerns a certain Mr. Ch'ou, a long-time political prisoner of the Kuomintang during the 1920s. At one point, he was to be executed, but the sentence was commuted after the intervention of his rich and highly respected family. He spent his years of idleness in prison, practicing meditation and consequently achieving a high level of enlightenment. After his eventual release from prison, he was recognized as a master and became quite famous, especially for his magical skill at divination. It is said that he could accurately recount a person's past and future destiny in great detail after meeting him only briefly—even perfect strangers. Unfortunately, however, while in Shanghai he became involved with a beautiful woman, a concubine of a defeated warlord, and his magic powers disappeared entirely.

Through such stories, one can glimpse the difficulty involved in achieving and maintaining hsienship. It clearly cannot be attained by sporadic means, but requires a constant commitment for one's entire life. This was expressed with great clarity by Lao Tzu, who wrote:[11]

> People in the conduct of their affairs often ruin them when they are on the very brink of success. If they were as careful at the end as at the beginning, they would not so ruin them.

NOTES

1. In *The Meditation Book of Sun Pu Er Niang* (available through True Beauty and Kindness Publishing Co., Taiwan).

2. *I Ching*, trans. James Legge, New York: Dover reprint of 1899 edition, p. 13. See also Richard Wilhelm and Cary F. Baynes, trans., Princeton University Press, 1967, pp. 382-83.

3. For another translation, see *The Texts of Taoism (TT)*, trans. James Legge, Oxford University Press, 1891, vol. 1, p. 83.

4. For another translation, see *ibid.*, p. 73.

5. Compare *ibid.*, pp. 53-54.

6. *Ibid.*, p. 171. See also *Tao Te Ching*, trans. L. Feng and J. English, New York: Random House, 1972, p. 12.

7. *Chuang Tzu*, ch. 11; *TT*, vol. 1, p. 299.

8. *Tao Te Ching*, ch. 33; *TT*, vol. 1, p. 75.

9. *Tao Te Ching*, ch. 55; *TT*, vol. 1, p. 99.

10. *TT*, vol. 1, p. 68.

11. *Tao Te Ching*, ch. 64; *TT*, vol. 1, p. 108.

CHAPTER 11

THE TAOIST GODS AND TEMPLES

In the last chapter we discussed hsienship, immortality. In this chapter we will speak about shen, or "god." In the Chinese language, shen has two meanings: god 神 and 魂 the spirit. It is different from kwei (ghost):

> The light spirits [shen] are outgoing; they are the active spirits which can also enter upon new incarnations. The dark spirits [kwei] return home; they are the withdrawing forces and have the task of assimilating what life has yielded.[1]

As we mentioned in the last chapter, in the Chinese character of hsien, the left side is a man and the right side a mountain. The ideogram is translated to mean "a man who practices the Taoist technique in the mountains." When such a man has achieved immortality, he is still a man but now is endowed with the spiritual power with which to transform himself into air and then to gather himself back into human form.

In order to be shen, a man may or may not practice the Taoist technique. He becomes shen if he has great virtue or ability, contributes something of great benefit to society, or dies in a war for the nation. After his death, either he is respected as a god or the government bestows on him the title of shen. In pre-Revolutionary China, people believed that the spirit of such a man continued to exist, that his great deeds would be remembered, and that his spiritual power could help them. There are many examples of this in Chinese history. The first was Hou T'u, an official of land or soil under the Yellow Emperor, Hwang Ti. After he died, he became known as a god of land and given the name She. Another was Hou Chi, who was the minister of agriculture and gave the people agricultural knowledge that helped them greatly. When he died, he was proclaimed the god of agriculture. These two gods became known as She-Chi. Altars erected in their name were established in the capital as well as the provinces. In the Li Chi (Book of Rites), the chapter on "The Rules of the Kings" says:

> The emperor offers oxen in sacrifice to She-Chi;
> Dukes sacrifice sheep as offerings to She-Chi.

The name of She-Chi always represents the country or the state. Food and the land are considered so fundamental to life that the writings of Mencius and Confucius mention She-Chi frequently. Similarly, numerous gods—such as the god of fire, the god of rain—memorialize people whose feats have benefited mankind. Emperor Kuang Hsu, second-to-last ruler of the Ch'in dynasty, reigned from 1875 to 1908. He plowed fields to commemorate the She-Chi ritual at what was then called Nung Hsien T'an (Temple of the Ancient Farmer).[2]

Another kind of god commemorates those who have died in wars, either in service to the nation or to protect society from disaster. The famous book *Feng Shen Yen I*—see chapter 7 above—systematically details a battle of the eleventh century B.C., between Chiang Tze-ya, a Taoist military strategist of the Chou dynasty, and Wen Chung, a general defending the corrupt Shang Yin dynasty. Although his forces were victorious, Chiang Tze-ya lost many men in battle—including even Taoists and volunteers from other religious sects who had fought alongside his enlisted army. To honor these dead soldiers and religious mercenaries, Chiang Tze-ya proclaimed that their spirits had become gods. Wen Chung finally died in this war and was deified as the god of thunder.[3]

In the generations after this event, those who died valiantly have likewise been awarded deification. The best known of these, Kuan Yü, was a general in the later Han dynasty ("Period of Three Kingdoms") 1,700 years ago. Kuan Yü was a brave warrior whose example was an inspiration to his men. When he refused to surrender in battle, he was captured by the enemy, the Kingdom of Wu, and put to death. In each generation that followed, more and more honors were bestowed on his memory, including his being proclaimed a god of war. Many public temples honor Kuan Yü; his portrait is displayed in many private homes and even some business organizations.

Other myths and legends about the lives of the gods are found in the popular Chinese classic *Hsi Yu Chi* (Journey to the West). This book has influenced Chinese society even more than the writings of Lao Tzu and Confucius. The educated are attracted by its beautiful poems and delicate lyrics, which augment the stories with verses in the terminology of Taoist and Buddhist meditation. And the peasants are so beguiled by tales of ghosts, demons, monsters, and fairies that those who cannot read recite its exciting legends during periods of work or recreation. The tales in *Hsi Yu Chi* have been the source of countless dramas, Chinese operas, and movies. Indeed, when the Performing Arts Ensemble of the People's Republic of China recently conducted a national tour in the United States, a highlight of their program was an excerpt from *The Monkey King Raises Havoc in Heaven*. According to *The New York Times* of July 2, 1978, this segment was very well received by American audiences.

The author of *Hsi Yu Chi* was the enlightened Taoist master Ch'iu Ch'u Chi, mentioned in previous chapters, who lived during the later Sung and the Yuan dynasties. So great was his reputation that Genghis Khan, notorious conqueror of half of Europe and the whole of Asia, invited him to the Great Snow Mountain in West Central Asia near Tibet. From Peking, Ch'iu Ch'u Chi had to travel very far, through Shing Kiang Province.

Hsi Yu Chi itself is about a long and arduous journey. Like Chaucer's *Canterbury Tales*, it is framed around a pilgrimage, but in this instance the journeyman, a master named Hsuan Chwang, travels alone. He is accompanied only by four celestial creatures: the monkey fairy, the pig fairy, the monk named Sha Ho-shang, and a powerful white steed. Departing from Ch'ang An, the pilgrim and his party are beset by steep mountains, tumultuous rivers, and desolate wastelands. Not only do they encounter savage beasts and poisonous snakes, but they must also combat fierce demons and monsters that can assume deceptive forms. *Hsi Yu Chi* records these adventurous travels.

The lives and ways of the gods are especially well described in its stories about the monkey fairy, Sung Wu-kung. This ferocious and cunning creature possesses supernatural powers and an impish sense of humor. Despite the supreme power of the Jade Emperor, the Ruler of Heaven, Sung Wu-kung's antics are a constant source of outrageous fun and adventure. But *Hsi Yu Chi* uses these stories for a serious purpose as well as for entertainment.

One function of these stories is to raise parallels between the mores of the gods and those of human society. Chapters 4 through 7 describe the Court of the Jade Emperor, replete with messengers, guards, officers, and fairy servants. The emperor has even domesticated animals, which comprise the stars in the heavens—including the dog, horse, swine, chicken, fox, and snake. Life in this court further resembles human society in that everyone has tasks to do. Some subjects tend the imperial peach garden, some ferment the celestial wine. These delicacies are served at elaborate banquets, where gods and fairies may be the guests, but the rituals and games of human banquets take place. As is the case on Earth, Taoist priests attend these fabulous feasts and participate in the festivities with other celestial guests.

The fragility of such a society, however, is also paralleled, thanks to the monkey fairy. At one time, the monkey fairy was angered when he learned that the Jade Emperor had handed out positions of rank to others but had neglected him. To appease Sung Wu-kung, the Jade Emperor gave him the title of Pi-ma Wen. This consoled the monkey fairy until he discovered that such an office required him to tend the celestial stables of the imperial horses.

But the monkey fairy really raised havoc in Heaven when the Jade Emperor excluded him from the guest list for a gala banquet. He sneaked before the feast was to begin and devoured all the imperial peaches and celestial wine. The peaches were endowed with the gift of immortality, but the wine still made him very drunk indeed. As he made his way home in a drunken stupor, he came upon one of Lao Tzu's treasures, a cache of pills which also assured immortality, which he swilled down as fast as he could. Thus the human foibles of envy and gluttony are present even in the most divine societies.

Now that the monkey fairy was twice-blessed with immortality, he caused more trouble around Heaven than ever before. He led his armies on many escapades, sometimes even defeating the forces of the Jade Emperor. Because he could change into seventy-two different forms, Sung Wu-kung caused great vexation and, even when captured, was able to escape. It appeared that nothing could be done to sway the monkey fairy from disrupting the order of Heaven with ever more misery and confusion. It is at this point that a second serious purpose of *Hsi Yu Chi* is illustrated: the advancement of accord between followers of Buddhism and those of Tao.

The monkey fairy at last considered himself so powerful that he declared himself monkey king and told the Jade Emperor to abdicate his throne. In desperation, the Taoist Divinity turned to Buddha, Jou-lai Fo, for help. Buddha demanded of the monkey king, "What is so special about you that you feel entitled to the emperor's throne?"

"I am the great immortal!" boasted the monkey king. "And I can change my shape so many ways that even the Jade Emperor cannot keep me prisoner! Why, I'm so great that with just one somersault I can travel a hundred and eight thousand li!" (thirty-six thousand miles).

Buddha held Sung Wu-kung in the palm of his hand and vowed, "If you can jump out of my hand in one leap, monkey king, I will acknowledge your claim to the Throne of Heaven and henceforth you can do whatever you desire."

The spritely fairy somersaulted in one giant leap across the vastness of Heaven until he reached the Five Great Red Pillars that mark the boundaries of the created Universe. To prove he had won, he unloaded a large pool of monkey piss at the base of the center Pillar and wrote on the side of the Pillar itself: "The monkey king was here!"

When he returned to the place where Jou-lai Fo was waiting for him, the monkey king boasted triumphantly that he had in fact leaped out of the palm of Buddha's hand. "True," admitted Buddha, "the stench of your urine still wreaks at the base of one of the Five Great Red Pillars. But behold the words you have written!" And with that, Buddha raised his middle finger to reveal the spot where the monkey king had written his name.

Then Buddha enclosed Sung Wu-kung in the giant palm of his hand and carried him out of Heaven. His five fingers became the five elements (earth, fire, water, metal, and wood), which Buddha instantly transformed into five adjoining mountains called Wu Hsing Shan. Here the monkey king remained imprisoned for five hundred years, until a Buddhist monk named Kuan Yin P'u-sa arranged suitable terms for his release. According to the conditions of his pardon, the monkey fairy would accompany the master Hsuan Chwang on a perilous pilgrimage.

We shall soon see how the punishment of the monkey king is a metaphor for a more sophisticated meaning. But it must also be seen that the fabulous adventures of Sung Wu-kung serve not only to thrill and delight but also encourage religious harmony between Buddhists and Taoists.

The third serious purpose of *Hsi Yu Chi* is to illustrate Taoist meditation techniques that can lead to immortality. The journey of master Hsuan Chwang and his four celestial creatures becomes, in this context, a profound philosophical metaphor.

Consider first the personality of the monkey king. He is impulsive and difficult to control. His supernatural powers permit him to soar to the heavens, race over the far reaches of the earth, and even explore the depths of the sea. But inhibited by so few restraints, he wants to do a hundred things at once. *Hsi Yu Chi* calls him the "heart monkey," for metaphorically he represents the emotional imagination. Emotions and ideas, too, wander wherever they will, since human thought is limitless and cannot be deterred by physical boundaries. The monkey fairy's ability to change into seventy-two different forms implies that the imagination is mutable, dwelling not in truth but in a realm of fantasy and dreams.

In the eight trigrams, the monkey represents Li, meaning "red, fire, and second daughter." The outer lines of the trigram are Yang; the inner ones, Yin. Therefore, the monkey's face is red and his behavior is mischievous (Yang), but his internal nature is feminine (Yin). This is fortunate, for otherwise he would no doubt rape and seduce many female fairies. The "kung" of Sung Wu-kung means "empty." In meditation, this means that the heart and the mind must be empty—that is devoid of passionate feeling, mischief, and illusion—before the path to immortality can be followed with success.

In this respect, Buddha's form of punishment for the monkey king relates to meditation. The five elements that imprison him serve as a metaphor for the five internal organs most vital to the human body: heart, kidney, lungs, stomach, and liver. Whereas the free, undisciplined imagination runs wild and lacks sufficient control, in meditation the Taoist buries the mind deep beneath the five internal organs where it resides, without distraction in the *tan t'ien*, which is located three inches below the navel.

The second celestial creature that accompanies Hsuan Chwang in the classic *Hsi Yu Chi* is Chu Pa-chieh, the pig fairy. In the eight trigrams, the pig represents K'an, meaning "black, water, and second son." Water is the element of the kidneys, signifying sexual energy. The "nun" of his Taoist name—Chu Wu-nun—likewise means energy. Like the imagination of the monkey fairy, the libido of the pig fairy lacks self-control, and his unchecked sexual appetites get him in trouble. In Chapter 18 of *Hsi Yu Chi*, the pig fairy marries a human girl, adopting human form. In Chapter 23, he wants to marry three young maidens and their mother as well! Such energy is vital but— like the imagination—lacks self-discipline and quietude.

Imagine, then, the problems that can result when the monkey fairy and the pig fairy combine forces! It is very important that control and harmony exist between the heart and the kidney, the imagination and the libido, fire and water. In meditation, this bond of accord between fire and water is called the union of K'an and Li. However, the frequent conflict between these spirits makes such harmony difficult to sustain.

This explains the importance of the third celestial traveler who accompanies Hsuan Chwang on his westward journey. In the eight trigrams, the monk Sha Ha-shang represents K'un (yellow and earth). His internal organ is the stomach. Like the earth, it is not so vigorous as fire and water (the imagination and the sexual appetite); instead it acts like a union arbitrator. It separates them physically and yet makes possible a more moderate bond between them. It is here that the *tan t'ien* holds the calmed and empty mind, buried beneath the stomach and the other internal organs.

The monkey fairy symbolizes the spirit, the pig fairy the sperm, and the monk the *ch'i* of breathing and vitality. The fourth creature symbolizes the final internal element necessary to meditation. The white charger represents the human will. Like the mighty steed, the will can be very strong but cannot achieve immortality all by itself. In fact, the four together—spirit, sperm, vitality, and will—are not enough to attain immortality through meditation on their own. They may be essential if the master is to succeed, but they also depend on the physical body of the master to serve as the medium of living meditation. For this reason, Hsuan Chwang is also important, for he represents the flesh and blood of a real human being. His dependence on the four celestial creatures—and theirs on him—combine in a united journey to eternal life.

Such a journey, of course, is fraught with obstacles that must not deter the master of meditation. In *Hsi Yu Chi*, Hsuan Chwang and his party travel sixty li (approximately twenty miles) each day. The journey takes fourteen years. The path is filled with physical hardships—such as severe heat and cold, steep mountains, and ravaging river currents. Lions and tigers, demons and monsters meet them at every turn. Some monsters recall the sirens of ancient Greek mythology, luring the traveler from the proper path. The obstacles threaten Hsuan Chwang's party with specific metaphorical emphasis. The impatient monkey must not fly ahead in the imagination but be content to proceed at a controlled and regular pace; the master's body must battle and withstand the relentlessness of physical hardship; the strength of the will must be harnessed to help him persevere; the voracious pig fairy must not succumb to his own appetites; and the monk must contain all in a spiritual equilibrium.

Even Buddhist monks have realized that the monsters described in *Hsi Yu Chi* are more than fairy tale fantasies. These monsters exist within the mind of the pilgrim. The truth of this insight is substantiated by yet another collection of Chinese myths and legends.

Recall the monkey king's arrogance, with which he declared himself superior to the Jade Emperor. Another name for the monkey king is Ch'i T'ien Ta Sheng: literally, Great Sage Equal to Heaven. Throughout China, he has been worshiped and revered by many as a powerful deity. As recently as the Boxer Rebellion, some religious societies and superstitious organizations invoked his power on their behalf. But the fourth volume of the seventeenth-century anthology *Liao Chai Chih I*, by P'u Sung-ling, accounts an older legend on this score.

Two brothers left their native city of Yen in Shantung Province in order to conduct business in distant Mien (today known as Fu-Chien Province). When they arrived at their lodgings, the innkeeper advised them to visit the local temple of a most powerful god, in order to assure their continued good fortune. Following his directions, the brothers arrived at a vast temple wherein many devout worshipers burned incense in prayer before a statue of the god. Sculpted in ornate finery was the body of a man with the head of a monkey. Shu Sheng, the younger brother, exclaimed, "This is no god! It's only the monkey fairy from the writings of Ch'iu Ch'u Chi! These fools are worshiping the personification of unbridled dreams!"

The idolators kneeling within earshot were scandalized by Shu Sheng's irreverence. News of his blasphemy spread so fast that the inn where they lodged was buzzing about it by the time the brothers returned there. The innkeeper gravely explained to the young man that his scorn had offended the powerful Ch'i T'ien Ta Sheng. Unless he repented, Shu Sheng would doubtless fall prey to disaster. "If disaster comes, it comes," retorted Shu Sheng. "But no matter what you say, it won't depend on whether or not I worship that fairy-tale god!"

In the middle of the night, Shu Sheng awoke with a throbbing pain in his head. His brother regarded this as the beginning of the monkey god's retribution and beseeched Shu Sheng to pray to Ch'i T'ien Ta Sheng for forgiveness. "I don't care what happens to me!" insisted Shu Sheng. "I won't pray to that monkey fairy if it kills me!" Immediately, the headache disappeared. But as suddenly an ulcer began to grow on the surface of his inner thigh. It swelled larger and larger, causing great pain and suffering to the young man. Only by atoning to the monkey god, he was told, could his affliction be cured. "Nonsense!" he persisted. "I need a surgeon, not a monkey fairy!"

A surgeon was summoned from among the people in that city. The ulcer was badly infected and grew worse with each passing moment. Skillful as he was, the surgeon extracted much blood and considerable quantities of pus from Shu Sheng's leg before the ulcer could be successfully removed. But as soon as the physician was finished, a new ulcer began to grow on Shu Sheng's other thigh, as quickly and as painfully as the first. The infection would not go away. Shu Sheng continued to be tormented.

But we should not conclude from this story that the torment suffered by Shu Sheng was the direct result of blasphemy. He was correct to reject the monkey god as a worthless superstition. Nonetheless, Shu Sheng was like many people. He possessed good sense and a strong will. However, his mind was not strong enough by itself to combat the superstitions and fears pressed on him by others. The human mind creates powerful gods. Unless a person is free of fantasy and illusion, he may still fall prey to these monsters of the imagination. The creatures described in *Hsi Yu Chi* are the product of Ch'iu Ch'u Chi's talent and should not be taken literally. It is when we approach them as metaphors that we can learn a great deal from them.

With this in mind, let us turn to yet another legendary aspect of Chinese culture: its ancient temples and man-made gods. From the ancient times until the formation of the Republic of China, all Chinese—from the emperor to the lowliest peasant—offered sacrifices and respect to Heaven (T'ien) and Earth (Ti), the rivers and mountains, and, especially, their ancestors. *The Book Of History (Shu Ching)* relates how Emperor Wu of the Chou dynasty, the son of King Wen, overthrew the Shang Yin dynasty. Like the forefathers of the American Revolution, he began his assault with an appeal to the people that Emperor Shin Shou was a tyrant. To support this serious charge, he claimed that Shin Shou failed to respect Heaven.[4] After triumphing over this corrupt and dissolute dynasty, he proclaimed his devotion to Heaven and Earth, famous mountains and great rivers.[5]

While many Chinese classics mention Heaven with great reverence, similar respect is expressed for mountains and rivers, as well as for the practice of sacrifice. This concept demonstrates a belief in the venerability of nature. Furthermore, it acknowledges the benefits afforded to human society by the fecundity of nature—such as grain, fuel, clothing, and so on. However, no special deity was associated with this reverence for nature until the emergence of Taoism in China.

According to Taoist teachings, each mountain and river is governed by a specially named god. For example, the religious pioneer Chang Tao Ling is still respected as a god at the Mountain of the Dragon and the Tiger (Lung Hu Shan) in Kiangsi Province. Similarly, T'ao Hung-ching is revered for ruling the Chu Yung Mountain. In most cases, each god practices Taoist meditation in the mountain region over which he reigns. Most Taoists practice their faith in the mountains, where these gods are considered to be immortal spirits of the Tao religion. While these deities have existed since the later years of the Han dynasty, more details about them appeared during the Sung dynasty. Hundreds of mountains and their gods are mentioned in the *Yuen Chi Ch'i Ch'ien.*

Ancestor worship has long been a traditional Chinese custom. Taoists, too, respected their ancestors like gods. This practice dates back to the Chou dynasty, when King Wu was very sick and near death. His brother Chi Tan, also known as the duke of Chou, built altars, made sacrifices, and wrote tablets of prayer to the spirits of his father King Wen, his grandfather King Chi, and his great-grandfather King T'ai.[6] This illustrates the great respect shown to ancestors as godlike spirits who could intercede to protect and aid their descendants. This tradition of ancestor worship is common to ancient Taoists and the Confucian *Book of History.*

Each Taoist temple is different in name from Buddhist temples. Taoists classify their temples according to four names: Kuan, Kung, Tien, and Koh.

Kuan is an *I Ching* hexagram ☴, which means "contemplation."

Traditionally, Kuan refers to a ritual in which the emperor ceremoniously washed his hands before worshiping his ancestors, with the judgment:

> Contemplation. The ablution has been made,
> But not yet the offering.
> Full of trust they look up to him.

However, Taoists apply the name to their temples to connote more religious and spiritual cleansing.

Ten miles from Peking, in the West Mountain, is situated the most famous temple bearing this name: Po Yuen Kuan (White Cloud Temple), which is considered headquarters of the Northern Taoist School. Erected during the Yuan dynasty (1277–1355), Po Yuen Kuan is the burial place and revered memorial for the enlightened Taoist master Ch'iu Ch'u Chi. On the thirteenth day of the eighth month in the Chinese calendar, Ch'iu Ch'u Chi's birthday, many people stay overnight at the temple to "meet god." Respecting it as a sacred shrine, many Taoist priests have worked at this temple.

Their head priest is very wise, but also enjoys tremendous political power. Situated so near the capital city of China, his temple has attracted frequent visits from members of the imperial family and from men in high office. Their generous donations have enriched the temple and adorned its grounds with most exquisite decorations. During the nineteenth century, a wily priest named Kao Tao-cheng headed the Order at Po Yuen Kuan. With the aid of a secret formula, he sold aphrodisiacs which won him even more favor among the rich and nobles of Peking. Even the head of the Eunuchs, Li Lian-ying, became his close ally, through whom he gained access to the empress, Tz'i Chih T'ai Hou. His power became so great that he not only partook in bribery and the sale of political appointments but even became involved with international spies.

The second name for Taoist temples is Kung, meaning "palace." It comes from the name of the heavenly estate wherein the spirit of Lao Tzu now resides, Tou Chuai Kung. Because of Lao Tzu's immense popularity as a pioneer in Tao, many temples are named Kung in his honor. Earlier chapters in the book have cited other famous Kung temples. For instance, Po Yü Chan, one of the five masters of the Southern Taoist School in the South Sung dynasty, resided at T'ai Yi Kung. The three immortal Mao brothers are worshiped at Shan Mo Kung. Their popularity has contributed to the naming of Kung for several temples in the Kiang Su province.

The third appellation for Taoist temples is Tien, which means "imperial hall." Recall that the first six chapters of *Hsi Yu Chi* (Journey to the West) mention with frequency the court of the Jade Emperor Yü Huang Ta Ti, who received and commanded his subordinates from Ling Shao Tien. Because Yü Huang Ta Ti is one of the Taoist triad—governing over heaven—many Taoist temples bear this name out of respect for him.

The fourth popular name for Taoist temples is Koh, meaning "cabinet room." The name refers to the chamber where the Taoist triad convene. A photo of Shan Ch'ing Koh of the Yuen Nan province can be found in Needham's *Science and Civilization in China*. As the text explains, Shan Ch'ing means "Taoist Triad"—the Jade Emperor, Lao Tzu, and Yuan-shih T'ien-tsun.

NOTES

1. *The I Ching or Book of Changes*, trans. Richard Wilhelm and Cary F. Baynes, Princeton University Press, 1967, p. 295.

2. For an illustration of the god She-Chi personally plowing the fields, see *Horizon* Magazine, Summer 1974, p. 219.

3. See E.T.C. Werner, *Myths and Legends of China*, New York: Arno Press, reprint of 1922 ed., p. 209.

4. *The Shu Ching or Book of Historical Documents*, trans. James Legge, *The Chinese Classics*, vol. 5, Hong Kong University Press, 1960, p. 284.

5. *Ibid.*, p. 312.

6. *Ibid.*, pp. 351–54.

CHAPTER 12

THE TAOIST RITUALS

Taoism is the source of all Chinese philosophies and religions. Like water, it yields and accommodates itself to the shape of its container. For this reason, the Taoist rituals and teachings evolve and change along with the mores and folkways of the Chinese people. Thus, Taoism holds greater significance for Chinese life and philosophy than Buddhism and Christianity, both of which were brought to China by foreigners.

The Chinese people have long practiced a family kinship system commonly referred to as Ts'i T'ang (Ancestor's Hall). The lineage of the Ts'i T'ang will often continue for many generations. The importance of such a kinship system cannot be overestimated, for devotion and homage to the family is paramount to the Chinese. Any dishonor or insult suffered by a member of the family represents a disgrace for both the individual and the entire family. People in Chinatowns throughout the contemporary Western world are deeply influenced by powerful clan associations. To commemorate the New Year or to celebrate an ancestor's birthday, the clans will perform rituals of worship and sacrifice, similar to the holidays practiced by Westerners on Christmas Day and New Year's Eve.

The Taoist system illustrates the Chinese tradition of ancestral devotion and worship. The Taoist members of the same generation form a fraternity of younger or older "brothers." The first word in the name retains their family surname. The middle name, however, is the Taoist word designating the members of that generation. For example, the three main characters in the novel *Hsi Yu Chi* (Journey to the West) share the middle name Wu, uniting them as brothers in the same spiritual family. The last word of the name is different for each person, serving the same purpose as first names in Western societies.

The first chapter of *Hsi Yu Chi* describes the monkey king's attempt to study with the great immortal master. The master told the monkey king that he would be in the tenth generation of their school. From the original generation there are twelve words which denote their lineage. The word for the tenth generation is Wu, which signifies awareness. The monkey king was given the name Sun Wu K'ung, meaning that he was aware of all that is empty. The concept and significance of emptiness is fundamental to both Buddhism and Taoism. The two companions of the monkey king were named Chu Wu Nêng and Sha Wu Ching.

As in the natural family, the Taoist calls his teacher Shih-Fu, the meaning of which is "teaching father." Other members of the teacher's generation are referred to as venerable uncles and aunts. The older generation of teachers share the name "teaching grandfather," "teaching grand uncle," and so on. Conversely, the older generations call the younger Taoist "son," "grandson," and so on. In accordance with Chinese practice, even if the Taoist is not a member of his school but deserves respect due to his age, he is called Tao-Chang, which means "senior Taoist." Other titles given to Taoists are Tao-Shih, "Taoist priest," and Hsiang-Jen, "immortal man."

Similarly, the female Taoists use the same system of identification for their Taoist generations. Unmarried female Taoists are called Tao-Ku (maiden), while married female Taoists are called Tao-P'o (mother). For example, in the third volume of the novel *Liao Chai Chih I* by P'u Sung-ling, the female Taoist generation was known as Yuen. In the story, a young man, Chen Yu Sheng, visiting Lu-Tzu An Temple, meets four young women Taoists named Po Yuen Sheng,

Liang Yuen Tung, Sheng Yuen Mien, and Chen Yuen Ch'i. Yuen is the Taoist name denoting the woman's Taoist generation, while the first and last names represent, respectively, the woman's surname and given name.

Taoists, Buddhists, and Confucians practiced discrimination when teaching their knowledge and techniques. They gave public lectures on the Tao in the daytime when anyone was allowed to attend. However, when it came time to pass on the most important and secret teachings, they always selected the best students and taught them secretly in the middle of the night. We can find this story in *The Journey to the West*. In the second chapter of this novel the great Taoist master who had a high seat on the altar gave a commentary on Taoism. Many people attended this seminar. Suddenly the Taoist master asked the spiritual monkey king, "What is your interest?" The monkey king replied that he wanted to learn the method to achieve longevity. The master offered several ways, but the monkey king refused to learn. The master became very angry and beat him three times on the head with a ruler. Since he was angry he turned his back on the monkey king. He crossed his hands behind his back and shut the door as he left the room to return to his residence. Many students blamed the monkey king for the master's departure and said, "You were too stupid." Nevertheless, although the other students and people laughed at him, the monkey king understood the master's real meaning. The monkey king got up in the middle of the night at three o'clock. He went to the back door of the master's residence and saw the door still open. He entered and saw the master sleeping on the bed. The monkey king kneeled down before the bed. The master awakened and asked him, "Why do you come here in the middle of the night?" The monkey king said, "You told me to come at three o'clock through the back door." The master was pleased that the monkey king had good intuition. He taught him all the magic spells. The monkey king could fly in the heavens and ride clouds everywhere. In one somersault he could travel 36,000 miles. He could transform himself into seventy-two different shapes (animals, stones, trees) and possessed all kinds of fighting techniques.

Likewise, the Buddhists also selected the most intelligent students and taught them privately in the middle of the night. It is said that the great Ch'an (Zen) master of the fifth generation, Hung Jen, taught his student, Hui Neng, in a rice mill in the middle of the night. Hui Neng became the master of the sixth Ch'an generation and lived from 638 to 713.[1]

Under the almond tree, Confucius taught many hundreds of students publicly, but he also had his secret teachings which were passed on orally to specially selected students. These teachings are now found in the book *Chung Yung* (The Doctrine of the Mean). The introduction to this book tells how Confucius' grandson Tze Tzu wrote the *Chung Yung*, fearing that there would be some error in the oral method of teaching, or that some important teaching would be forgotten. He passed this knowledge on to Mencius who became the next great sage in the Confucian school.[2]

In the Taoist school, male and female students learn meditations and hymns. Besides this, they are also taught how to play various musical instruments, which are used in the Taoist rituals and ceremonies. Their services, employed by the public or a private family, entail ceremonies and prayers to revive the sick and avert calamity, as well as sacrifices and libations to gods, demons, or the dead. This kind of practice is illustrated in the thirteenth chapter of *Hung Lo Meng* (Dream of the Red Chamber), as the Chia family employs the services of forty-nine Taoists for the burial ceremony of Ch'in K'o Ch'ing. This young woman is the wife of Chia Yung, descendant of the Eastern branch of the Chia family. She is not only pretty but also friendly to everyone. Even the servants like her. Therefore, her family spends a great sum of money for her funeral ceremony. The forty-nine Taoists perform seven ceremonies, one every seven days after her death, for a total period of forty-nine days. These ceremonies are thought to make the spirit of the dead person more peaceful and free from disturbance by evil ghosts and demons.

When a middle-class person dies, the departed person's family employs one or more Taoists to give a ceremony from one to three days in length depending on the family's finances. The Taoists play musical instruments and speak magic sayings. It is believed that this service can benefit the dead person even if the deceased had sinned in his life. By virtue of the ceremony he can be excused from punishment by the gods.

During the ceremony the Taoist uses vermilion to write the dead person's name, birthdate, address, and date of death on two yellow papers. The seal of the Taoist temple is inscribed on the yellow papers. These papers resemble the Western certificate of death. One of these papers is put in the coffin and the other is burned. The belief is that the deceased person can go directly to the gods without being detained by the local spirits. As the coffin goes to the burial grounds, the Taoists walk in front of the coffin, shaking bells, playing musical instruments, saying magic spells. They believe they can guide the spirit of the deceased as he leaves his home and enters the graveyard. This kind of service is still practiced in Nationalist China.

Another kind of ceremony is that which is performed to drive evil ghosts or monsters from a place outdoors or in the home. The ghosts make strange noises or appear in ugly shapes and must be driven away because they can make people sick by their presence. A description of this service can also be found in *The Dream of the Red Chamber*, Chapter 102. The Chia family owns a garden called Ta Kuan Yuan (Great View Garden) which covers many acres. The garden has high hills and is crossed by streams and dotted with lakes. There are many kinds of trees, flowering plants, animals, and birds. It is a huge place, but only a few people live in its various buildings, more women than men. Sometimes the people hear strange voices in the hills and forests. They become afraid to go out at night. Some of the women become sick and begin to talk among themselves of their fears. They fear that ghosts are causing these disturbances. Finally it is decided to invite the Taoists to Ta Kuan Yuan to perform a service so that it might become peaceful once again.

The Chia family again employs forty-nine Taoists led by three Taoist priests to perform this service. Each of the priests wears a hat decorated with seven stars and a robe bearing the symbols of the eight trigrams and the T'ai Chi symbol. At the start of the ceremony five Taoists take five flags—green, red, yellow, white, and black—and stand in the five different directions: east, south, middle, west, and north. Then they hang portraits of the triad of Taoist gods. Next they burn incense and draw water from the well for magical use. When these things have been done, the Taoists begin to play all sorts of Taoist musical instruments, including drums and bells. One of the three priests takes a sword and the water. Another priest holds up a black banner decorated with seven stars. The third one takes a whip made of peachwood to drive the evil ghosts away. They invoke many gods and heavenly generals to catch the evil ghosts and monsters.

The forty-nine Taoists continue to wave the flags and play the musical instruments. Then, with the help of the gods and heavenly generals, they walk through the garden like a patrol. They pass through the hills and forests and enter every building. At last they declare they have caught many ghosts and monsters and have put them into different jars. The jars are sealed and magic spells are written on them to prevent the ghosts from escaping. When the ceremony is completed, peace again enters Ta Kuan Yuan.

The Taoist does not only perform services for the dead and inhabitants of the ghost world. There are also many practices which relate to children. A Taoist male or female may be designated the godfather or godmother of a newborn baby. It is believed that this will help the child to be safe and peaceful. In Chapter 25 of *The Dream of the Red Chamber*, the Taoist Ma Tao P'o is mentioned as the godmother of the young man Chia Pao Yu, who is the main character in the book.

Taoists believe in fate, that everything is determined by destiny: They believe the stars can be used to predict the destiny of a newborn child. Each star has a god, and by the motion of the earth, each god takes a turn "on duty." By the position of the stars, good fortune and misfortune can be determined.

Children can be troubled by many difficulties in the early period of their lives. There is always the possibility the child will fall in a well, be bitten by a snake, eaten by a tiger, or suffer any one of numerous calamities. The Taoists believe that the birthdate determines which of these difficulties is likely to beset a particular child. They then can provide a magic spell or create a charm or talisman to protect the child. This type of magic is popular in China, and some illustrations can be found in *The Dream of the Red Chamber*. In Chapter 29, the Chang Taoist gives a talisman to the daughter of Mrs. Chia Wong Shi Feng. Each year the daughter receives a new charm for her protection. In Chapter 62, the birthday of the young man Chia Pao Yu is celebrated. The Chang Taoist presents him with a scroll inscribed with his name and a magic spell. He is also told of the star that will govern his destiny for that year.

The Taoist is also called upon to help the sick. By using predictive techniques the Taoist can tell the sick person why he got sick, when he will begin to get better, and when he will be completely cured. An illustration of this type of practice can be found in *The Dream of the Red Chamber*, Chapter 102.

It is also possible for people to receive clues to their destiny by going to the Taoist temple. After praying to the gods, the person draws a slip (ch'ien) from a bamboo tube. Each slip gives a reference number to the Book of Divination by Lots. In Chapter 101 of *The Dream of the Red Chamber*, Mrs. Chia Wong Shi Feng is sick and goes to the temple to pray. She draws a lot and is referred to #33 in the *Book of Divination by Lots*. She is very surprised to see the subtitle: "Wong Shi Feng Returns to Birthplace Wearing Fine Dress." The #33 also contains a poem which says:

> He leaves his native place for twenty years.
> Now, wearing fine dress, he will return to the home and garden...

Mrs. Chia Wong Shi Feng, having no plans to visit her birthplace, thinks this prediction is very unlikely. But years later, when she dies, her coffin is returned to her native place to be buried.

Evidence of these practices is still found today in Chinatown. One may go to the Buddhist or Taoist temple and pay a small sum of money to draw a roll of paper with a message on it. And, of course, the famous fortune cookie uses this very same idea.

We have spoken of the types of services performed by Taoists for private families. Taoists are also hired by citizens' organizations to perform public services or celebrations at various times during the year. On the fifteenth day of the seventh month (August) falls the Chung Yuan festival. It is a festival to help the many ghosts that the Taoists believe are everywhere. Some ghosts have drowned in the river. If they are not helped, their spirits will always be under water. Some ghosts are hungry, so they are given food to eat. Both the Buddhists and the Taoists celebrate this festival. They use paper to make boats and place burning candles in them. These paper boats are put on the river while the Taoists and Buddhists chant magic spells.

The Taoists cover their faces with their hair. One hand holds a sword and the other holds a magic gavel. At the same time they spread cooked rice around everywhere. They believe this service enables the hungry ghosts to get food and the drunken ghosts to escape from the water. Then, they can enter reincarnation and will not cause any more trouble for the people.

Another festival day is the first day of the tenth month (November). It is called Hsia Yuan. In that the purpose of this festival day is to drive away ghosts and monsters, it is similar to Halloween. Some people pretend to be ghosts by wearing masks. The Taoist master takes a sword and says a magic spell. Other Taoists with swords chase the ghosts away. After this service, the place where it was held becomes more peaceful.

Taoist ideas have encouraged people to perform ceremonies of their own, that is, without any help from priests. On the 23rd or 24th day of the 12th month (January), a farewell party is given to send off the god of the kitchen. The god of the kitchen is on his way to heaven, where he will make his annual report to the Jade Emperor. This report tells whether a family did good or bad in the preceding year. The god of heaven makes a record for each person. According to this, they get either punishment or reward. On this day the people offer incense, candy, dishes of food, paper horses, and other sacrifices to the god of the kitchen. The candy is made of a special, very sticky, gumlike sugar. The purpose of these sacrifices is to ensure he will only say good things to the god of heaven. The people kneel down to pray and say, "When you go to heaven you should report only good things, and when you come down from heaven you should protect us and bring peace and safety to us." This celebration commemorates the time that Wang Sun Chia asked Confucius who he thought it was better to flatter: the kitchen god or the god of mystery.[3]

Another Chinese ritual or festival day is called Ch'ing Ming. It is celebrated within a few days of Christian Palm Sunday and Jewish Passover, but its purpose is closer to that of Easter. Between April 4 and 6, families travel out to the cemetery to honor their ancestors and repair their tombs. They add soil around the base of the grave, burn incense, and offer wine and food to the spirits of their loved ones. Into the fire they place paper bills called "ghost money." The wails of grief-stricken mourners at some gravesides suggest that the deceased has just recently died. Kao Chü Ch'ing, a great poet of the Sung dynasty, depicts this scene as follows:

> Hills to the north and south contain many graves.
> During the Clear and Bright Festival,
> Many are occupied with repairing ancestral tombs.
> Ashes of ghost money spiral skyward like white butterflies.
> Tears flow like blood, the color of red flowers.

Ch'ing Ming is not merely a time of grieving and repair. It is also a time of family togetherness and festivity. Families cut branches from willow trees and place them in their doorways, much as Christians carry palm branches on Palm Sunday. Their journey together out to the gravesites becomes an event that somewhat resembles the festivity of the Easter Parade.[4] Even in bad weather, this can be a special time—as suggested by the poet Tu Mu, also of the T'ang dynasty:

> Travelers along the road are upset by constant rain.
> They ask the cowboy where to find wine.
> He points the way to a village among almond blossoms.

This painting is a thirty-foot long scroll depicting various phenomena of society in Kai Fen, capital of the Sung dynasty. Among other things it shows the river and land, bridges and boats, and different members of the society—nobles, officials, traders, workers, and so on.

The people perform many such ceremonies during the year. They celebrate various events such as the birthday of the Jade Emperor. A list of these celebrations is given at the end of this chapter.

It is hard to say whether these Taoist services really have magical power or if it is the creation of a psychological effect that is important. However, some Taoists overly propagandize their powers for business purposes.

There once was a Taoist priest who always boasted of his spiritual power and magical abilities to drive away ghosts and catch evil spirits. He said his power was so strong that he employed ghosts for his servants. His arrogance was not appreciated by some of his neighbors, and one day, as the Taoist was on his way to a nearby village for the purpose of exorcising some troublesome ghosts, a mischievous young man saw the perfect opportunity to teach this Taoist magician a lesson.

After the successful completion of his ceremony, for which he was well paid, the Taoist headed back to his own village, carrying his horn and bells, the instruments of his profession. His attention was suddenly attracted by a strange voice from a tree along side the road. He looked up and saw a most fearsome ghost. Still believing in his magic power, he blew his horn and shook his bells, but the creature, with his fiery red eyes and bushy purple mane was not deterred. He continued to advance toward the Taoist, who, giving up on his magic power, had begun to run.

The Taoist, propelled by fear, soon neared his home. He was badly shaken and very tired from running. He collapsed outside his gate, almost dead. His family, hearing the disturbance, brought him into the house.

The next day he was reluctant to speak of his experience. He took a walk outside his house and found his horn and bells hanging high in a tree. From that day on, he never boasted of his magic power again.

List of Festivals

Chinese Month	Day	Festival
1st (February)	1st	Birthday of Yuan-shih T'ien-tsun (one of the Taoist Triad of Gods)
	4th	Birthday of Heavenly Medicine Doctor Sun Chen Jen
	9th	Birthday of Jade Emperor (one of the Taoist Triad of Gods)
	15th	Birthday of God of the Door
2nd (March)	2nd	Birthday of God of Fortune and Virtue
	3rd	Birthday of God of Literature

	15th	Birthday of Lao Tzu (one of the Taoist Triad of Gods, Pioneer of Taoism)
	19th	Birthday of Kuan Shih Yin (female god in Taoism and Buddhism)
3rd (April)	5th	Clear and Bright (Ch'ing Mien)
	15th	Birthday of Emperor Wu Chen Jen, Protector of Life
	15th	Birthday of General Chao, God of Treasure
	19th	Birthday of God of Sun
	23rd	Birthday of Sheng Mu, Heavenly Sage Mother
	26th	Birthday of Kuei Ku Tze
	28th	Birthday of Great Emperor of Eastern Mountain
4th (May)	14th	Birthday of Lu Tzu (Lu Tung Pin)
	18th	Birthday of Purple Emperor of North Star
	18th	Birthday of Hwa T'o, Medicine Doctor
	21st	Birthday of Heavenly Emperor Li
	28th	Birthday of Shen Nung, Divine Husbandman
5th (June)	1st	Birthday of Longevity King of South Star
	13th	Birthday of Kuan Yü, Sage King
6th (July)	15th	Birthday of Spiritual Heaven King Wong
	19th	Kuan Shih Yin Achieves the Tao
	24th	Birthday of God of Thunder
7th (August)	15th	Birthday of Chung Yuan, God of Earth
	18th	Birthday of Western Queen Mother
8th (September)	3rd	Birthday of God of the Kitchen
9th (October)	9th	Birthday of King of the Ghost World
10th (November)	12th	Birthday of Monkey King
	15th	Birthday of God of Water
	18th	Birthday of Earth Mother
	25th	Birthday of Shu Chen Jen
11th (December)	15th	Winter Solstice
12th (January)	23–24th	Kitchen God Goes to Heaven
	25th	Heavenly Gods Come to Human Society

NOTES

1. Fung Yu Lan, *History of Chinese Philosophy*, et. Derk Bodde, Princeton: Princeton University Press, 1953, pp. 387–393. New York: Free Press, 1966.

2. *The Doctrine of the Mean*, in *The Chinese Classics (CC)*, trans. James Legge, Hong Kong University Press, 1960, vol. 1, p. 382.

3. See *CC*, vol. 1, p. 159.

4. A famous Chinese painting "Ch'ing Ming Ho Shang T'u" (Ch'ing Ming Day along the Banks of the River) appears in *Horizon* Magazine, vol. 9, no. 2, Spring 1972, p. 30.

index